Penguin International Poets

Octavio Paz: Selected Poems

Octavio Paz, born in Mexico City in 1914, is one of the major poets of Latin America. In 1937 he visited the Republican zone in Spain, and on his return to Mexico founded a literary review, *Taller*, which gathered together the young Mexican and Spanish writers of the time. He lived in the United States from 1943 to 1945, at which time he joined the Mexican diplomatic service, and then a series of posts kept him abroad for many years. In 1949 he published his first important collection of poems, *Libertad bajo palabra*, and the following year his well-known essay on Mexico, *El laberinto de la soledad* (*Labyrinth of Solitude*), which has been translated into almost every European language. *¿Aguila o sol?* (1951, *Eagle or Sun?*), poetry and prose, comes closest to surrealism of all his works.

In 1955 Paz published *El arco y la lira* (The Bow and the Lyre), essays on poetics, and one of his major poems, 'Piedra de sol', also extensively translated, appeared in 1959. He was appointed Ambassador to India in 1962, and during his stay there became absorbed in Oriental art and philosophy. He published two collections of poetry, *Salamandra* (1962) and *Ladera este* (1969), the latter encompassing his Eastern experiences. A prolific prose writer, he has written essays on anthropology, aesthetics and politics, some of which are collected in *Corriente alterna* (*Alternating Current*) and *Conjunciones y disyunciones* (*Conjunctions and Disjunctions*).

Paz resigned his post in India in 1968, in protest against the Mexican government's massacre of students in Mexico City in that year. In 1970 he taught at Cambridge, and in 1971 returned to Mexico and founded *Plural*, a magazine of art, literature, criticism and politics, which had a profound influence on Latin American intellectual life. Due to government intervention, Paz and the editorial board of *Plural* resigned in 1976 and founded another monthly publication, *Vuelta*, which continues the cultural and critical work begun by its predecessor. Since then Paz has published *Vuelta* (poems) and various books of essays, including his book on Marcel Duchamp, *La apariencia desnuda* (*Marcel Duchamp: Appearance Stripped Bare*). His most recent work is *The Monkey Grammarian*.

Octavio Paz won the International Poetry Grand Prix in 1963 and the Jerusalem Prize in 1977. In 1990 he was awarded the Nobel Prize for literature.

Selected Poems

OCTAVIO PAZ

Edited by Charles Tomlinson

PENGUIN BOOKS

PENGUIN BOOKS

Published by the Penguin Group
Penguin Books Ltd, 27 Wrights Lane, London w8 5TZ, England
Viking Penguin, a division of Penguin Books USA Inc.
375 Hudson Street, New York, New York 10014, USA
Penguin Books Australia Ltd, Ringwood, Victoria, Australia
Penguin Books Canada Ltd, 2801 John Street, Markham, Ontario, Canada L3R 1B4
Penguin Books (NZ) Ltd, 182–190 Wairau Road, Auckland 10, New Zealand

Penguin Books Ltd, Registered Offices: Harmondsworth, Middlesex, England

This selection first published 1979
10 9 8 7 6 5 4 3 2

'Introduction: A Note on Octavio Paz' copyright © Charles Tomlinson, 1979
'Poetry and History' by Octavio Paz from *Anthology of Mexican Poetry* copyright
© Thames & Hudson Ltd, 1959
The Acknowledgements on p. 11-12 constitute an extension of the copyright page
All rights reserved

Printed in England by Clays Ltd, St Ives plc
Set in Monotype Bembo

Contents

Contents

From *Vuelta* (1976)

Epilogue

From *Vuelta* (1976)

Epilogue

Editor's Foreword

The present collection consists mostly of Paz's later work. A selection of previous poems, with translations, is to be found in *Early Poems 1935–1955* (edited by Muriel Rukeyser and published by New Directions, 1973) and some of the later poems, also with translations, in *Configurations* (New Directions and Cape, 1971). The Spanish text of *Salamandra* and *Ladera este* is that published by Joaquín Mortiz; the text of *La estación violenta* that of *Early Poems*; the text of *¿Aguila o sol?* – except for two small revisions – is that of *Libertad bajo palabra, Obra poética (1935–1957)* (Fondo de Cultura Económica, 1968). Poems subsequent to *Ladera este* are from the author's own manuscripts. These, with the exception of 'Día', have now appeared in *Vuelta* (Seix Barral, 1976). The choice of poems was made in collaboration with Señor Paz.

CHARLES TOMLINSON

The translations are by Elizabeth Bishop, Paul Blackburn, Enrique Caracciolo-Trejo, Michael Edwards, Jack Hill, Lysander Kemp, Michael Schmidt, Arthur Terry, Charles Tomlinson, Eliot Weinberger, William Carlos Williams. 'Poetry and History' (p. 15) is translated by Samuel Beckett.

Acknowledgements

Poems from *La estación violenta:* published in the USA in *Early Poems 1935-1955* by New Directions Publishing Corporation 1973 (originally published as *Selected Poems* by Indiana University Press 1963)
Copyright © New Directions Publishing Corporation, 1973
Copyright © Octavio Paz and Jean Miller Blackburn, 1959
Copyright © Octavio Paz and Lysander Kemp, 1959
Copyright © Octavio Paz and Florence H. Williams, 1973
Acknowledgement is made to Fondo de Cultura Económica, Mexico, for permission to reprint the Spanish text from the volume *Libertad bajo palabra, Obra poética (1935-1957)*, 1960

Poems from *¿Aguila o sol?*: published in the USA in *Eagle or Sun?* by New Directions Publishing Corporation 1976
Copyright © 1960 by Fondo de Cultura Económica
Copyright © Octavio Paz and Eliot Weinberger, 1969, 1970, 1975, 1976
Acknowledgement is made to Fondo de Cultura Económica, Mexico, for permission to reprint the Spanish text from the volume *Libertad bajo palabra, Obra poética (1935-1957)*, 1960

Poems from *Salamandra*: published in the USA by New Directions Publishing Corporation and in Great Britain by Jonathan Cape in *Configurations* 1971
Copyright © New Directions Publishing Corporation, 1971
Copyright © Octavio Paz and Charles Tomlinson, 1968
Acknowledgement is made to Editorial Joaquín Mortiz, Mexico, for permission to reprint the Spanish text of the poems

Poems from *Ladera este*: 'El Mausoleo de Humayun', 'Pueblo', 'Felicidad en Herat', 'Juventud', 'Lo idéntico', 'Tumba del poeta', 'Aparición' 'Vrindaban' and 'Viento entero' published in the USA by New Directions Publishing Corporation and in Great Britain by Jonathan Cape in *Configurations* 1971
Copyright © New Directions Publishing Corporation, 1971
Copyright © Octavio Paz and Paul Blackburn, 1970
Copyright © Octavio Paz and Lysander Kemp, 1967
Copyright © Octavio Paz and Charles Tomlinson, 1968
'La higuera religiosa' and 'Cerca del Cabo Comorín' copyright © Octavio Paz and Arthur Terry, 1979
'En los jardines de los Lodi' and 'Efectos del bautismo' copyright ©

Introduction: A Note on Octavio Paz

'To possess truth in one soul and body.' Rimbaud's ideal might also be said to lie behind the post-Christian, post-Nietzschean poetry of Octavio Paz, with its search for innocence, its exploration of the time that love establishes within time, and its attempts to reach through and beyond dualism. Bakunin and parts of Blake anticipate the social implications of his work – implications, not formulations. For Paz insists on the non-ideological nature of poetry. 'Poetry is the *other* voice,' he writes. 'Not the voice of history or of anti-history, but the voice which, in history, is always saying something different.' This refusal of ideological servitude recalls André Breton and the surrealists in whose activities Paz participated. Indeed, one of the labels which stuck designates him 'a telluric surrealist'. But this oversimplifies the intellectual nature of his work, ignoring his debt to seventeenth-century Spanish baroque – particularly to Góngora and Quevedo – and his reading in medieval Spanish poetry. Among twentieth-century influences, besides Jorge Guillén, perhaps the moral presence and friendship of Luis Cernuda come foremost. He shares with Cernuda a bent towards French culture (towards Apollinaire, Reverdy, Breton), and an enthusiasm for Blake, Coleridge and the German romantics, especially Novalis. Among the romantic generation, Paz has turned most recently to Wordsworth. The French symbolists – Nerval (whom he translated), Baudelaire, Rimbaud and, later, Mallarmé – have all left their mark. Paz also admires Eliot – the Eliot of *The Waste Land*, a poem which for him is analogous to Mallarmé's *Un Coup de Dés* with its spatial and musical structure. If Eliot's 'moments in and out of time' seem to invite comparison with Paz, it should be recalled that in the latter what we experience is less an 'interpenetration of the timeless with time' than a deepening – often erotic – of the content of time itself.

For many years a diplomat, Paz writes an international poetry that has felt the changes of scene: Spain (during the civil war), the U.S.A., France, Japan, India, Britain. The East counts for much in his work: the literature of China and Japan discovered through Pound, Waley and Keene (he was himself to translate Basho); India from his years as ambassador in Delhi; Buddhism investigated simultaneously with a re-encounter with the work of Mallarmé. And in the art of India (above all the sculpture of Kārlī) he admires that combination of ecstasy and gravity which, in another form, characterizes much of his own mature poetry. Since his return to Mexico in 1971, Paz has written a number of poems of tragic intensity. One of the events which has deeply affected the later work of this, the most significant living poet of Latin America, is his marriage in 1964 to Marie-José Tramini.

CHARLES TOMLINSON

Poetry and History

Every poem is an attempt to reconcile history and poetry for the benefit of poetry. The poet always seeks to elude the tyranny of history even when he identifies himself with the society in which he lives, and when he participates in what is called 'the current of the age' – an extreme case which is becoming less and less imaginable in the modern world. All great poetic experiments – from the magic formula and the epic poem to automatic writing – claim to use the poem as a melting-pot for history and poetry, fact and myth, colloquialism and imagery, the date which can never be repeated and the festivity, a date which is alive and endowed with a secret fertility, ever returning to inaugurate a new period. The nature of a poem is analogous to that of a Fiesta which, besides being a date in the calendar, is also a break in the sequence of time and the irruption of a present which periodically returns without yesterday or tomorrow. Every poem is a Fiesta, a precipitate of pure time.

The relationship between men and history is one of slavery and dependence. For if we are the only protagonists of history, we are also its raw material and its victims: it can only be fulfilled at our expense. Poetry radically transforms this relationship; it can only find fulfilment at the expense of history. All its products – the hero, the assassin, the lover, the allegory, the fragmentary inscription, the refrain, the oath; the involuntary exclamation on the lips of the child at play, the condemned criminal, the girl making love for the first time; the phrase borne on the wind, the shred of a cry – all these, together with archaism, neologism, and quotation, will never resign themselves to dying, or to being battered against the wall. They are bent on attaining to the end, on existing to the utmost. They extricate themselves from cause and effect. They wait for the poem which will rescue them and make them what they are. There can be no poetry without history, but poetry has no other mission than to transmute history. And therefore the only true revolutionary poetry is apocalyptic poetry.

Poetry is made out of the very substance of history and society – language. But it seeks to re-create language in accordance with laws other than those which govern conversation and logical discourse. This poetic transmutation occurs in the innermost recesses of the language. The phrase – and not the isolated word – is the cell, the simplest element of language. A word cannot exist without other words, a phrase without other phrases.

That is to say, every sentence always contains an implicit reference to another, and is susceptible of explanation by another. Every phrase constitutes a 'wish to say' something, referring explicitly to something beyond it. Language is a combination of mobile and interchangeable symbols, each indicating 'towards' what it is going. In this way both meaning and communication are based on the 'intentionality' of words. But no sooner does poetry touch them than they are changed into rhythmic units or into images; they stand on their own and are sufficient unto themselves. Words suddenly lose their mobility; there are various ways of saying a thing in prose; there is only one in poetry. The poetical word has no substitute. It is not a *wish to say something*, but is something *irrevocably said*. Or alternatively, it is not a 'going towards' something, nor a 'speaking' of this or that. The poet does not speak of horror or of love: he shows them. Irrevocable and irreplaceable, the words of poetry become inexplicable except in terms of themselves. Their meaning is no longer beyond, but within them; the image is 'in' the meaning.

The proper function of the poetic image is to resolve into a unity realities which appear to us conflicting and irreducible. And this operation takes place without removing or sacrificing the conflicts and antagonisms between the entities which it evokes and re-creates. That is why the poetic image is inexplicable in the strict sense of the term. Now poetic language partakes of the ambiguity with which reality reveals itself to us. In transmuting the language, the image not only opens the door to reality, it also, as it were, strips reality bare and shows it to us in its final unity. The phrase becomes an image. The poem is a single image, or an indivisible constellation of images. The void left by the disappearance of what we call reality is peopled with a crowd of heterogeneous or conflicting visions, inevitably seeking to resolve their discord into a solar system of allusions – the poem: a universe of opaque, corruptible words which can yet light up and burn whenever there are lips to touch them. At certain times, in the mouths of some speakers, the phrase-mill becomes a source of evident truths requiring no demonstration. Then we are transported into the fullness of time. By exploiting language to the utmost the poet transcends it. By emphasizing history, he lays it bare and shows it for what it is – time.

When history allows us to suspect that it is perhaps no more than a ghostly procession, without meaning or end, ambiguity of language becomes more marked and prevents any genuine dialogue. Words lose their meaning, and thereby their power to communicate. The degradation of history into a mere sequence of events involves the degradation of language, too, into a collection of lifeless symbols. All men use the same words, but they do not understand one another. And it is useless for men to try to 'reach an agreement' on the meanings of words. Language is not a convention, but a dimension from which man cannot be separated. Every verbal adventure is total; a man stakes his whole self and life on a single word. The poet is a man whose very being becomes one with his words. Therefore, only the poet can make possible a new dialogue. The destiny of the poet, particularly in a period such as ours, is 'donner un sens plus pur aux mots de la tribu'. This implies that words are rooted out of the common language and brought to birth in a poem. What is called hermeticism of modern poetry springs from that fact. But words are inseparable from men. Consequently, poetic activity cannot take place outside the poet, in the magic object represented by the poem; rather does it take man himself as the centre of its experience. Opposites are fused in man himself, not in the poem alone. The two are inseparable. The poems of Rimbaud are Rimbaud himself, the adolescent fencing with shining blasphemies, despite all attempts to convert him into a kind of brute upon whom the word descended. No, *the poet and his word are one*. Such has been, during the past hundred years, the motto of the greatest poets of our civilization. Nor has the meaning of that last great movement of the century – surrealism – been any different. The grandeur of these attempts – to which no poet worthy of the name can be indifferent – lies in their endeavour to destroy once and for all, and in desperation, the dualism which tears us asunder. Poetry leaps into the unknown, or it is nothing.

In present circumstances, it may seem ludicrous to refer to the extravagant claims of poetry. Never has the domination of history been greater than now, never has the pressure of 'events' been so suffocating. In proportion as the tyranny of 'what to do next' becomes more and more intolerable – since our consent has not been asked for the doing, and since it is almost always directed towards man's destruction – so does poetic activity become more secret, isolated, and rare. Only yesterday, to write a poem or to fall in love were subversive activities, compromising the social order by exposing its double character. Today, the very notion of order has disappeared, and its place has been taken by a combination of forces, masses, and resistances. Reality has cast aside its disguises and contemporary society is seen for what it is: a heterogeneous collection of things 'homogenized' by the whip or by propaganda, directed by groups distinguishable from one another only by their degree of brutality. In these circumstances, poetic creation goes into hiding. If a poem is a Fiesta, it is one held out of season, in unfrequented places – an underground festivity.

But poetic activity is rediscovering all its ancient subversive powers by this very secrecy, impregnated with eroticism and the occult, a challenge to an interdict not less condemnatory for not being explicitly formulated. Poetry, which yesterday was required to breathe the free air of universal communion, continues to be an exorcism for preserving us from the sorcery of force and of numbers. It has been said that poetry is one of the means by which modern man can say *No* to all those powers which, not content with disposing of our lives, also want to rule our consciences. But this negation carries within it a *Yes* which is greater than itself.

OCTAVIO PAZ

(From *Anthology of Mexican Poetry*, Thames & Hudson, 1959.)

from *La estación violenta* (1948–57)

Himno entre ruinas

donde espumoso el mar siciliano . . .
                                        Góngora

Coronado de sí el día extiende sus plumas.
¡Alto grito amarillo,
caliente surtidor en el centro de un cielo
imparcial y benéfico!
Las apariencias son hermosas en esta su verdad momentánea.
El mar trepa la costa,
se afianza entre las peñas, araña deslumbrante;
la herida cárdena del monte resplandece;
un puñado de cabras es un rebaño de piedras;
el sol pone su huevo de oro y se derrama sobre el mar.
Todos es dios.
¡Estatua rota,
columnas comidas por la luz,
ruinas vivas en un mundo de muertos en vida!

Cae la noche sobre Teotihuacán.
En lo alto de la pirámide los muchachos fuman marihuana,
suenan guitarras roncas.
¿Qué yerba, qué agua de vida ha de darnos la vida,
dónde desenterrar la palabra,
la proporción que rige al himno y al discurso,
al baile, a la ciudad y a la balanza?
El canto mexicano estalla en un carajo,
estrella de colores que se apaga,
piedra que nos cierra las puertas del contacto.
Sabe la tierra a tierra envejecida.

Los ojos ven, las manos tocan.
Bastan aquí unas cuantas cosas:
tuna, espinoso planeta coral,
higos encapuchados,
uvas con gusto a resurrección,
almejas, virginidades ariscas,
sal, queso, vino, pan solar.
Desde lo alto de su morenía una isleña me mira,

Hymn among the Ruins

Where foams the Sicilian sea ...
                              Góngora

Self crowned the day displays its plumage.
A shout tall and yellow,
impartial and beneficent,
a hot geyser into the middle sky!
Appearances are beautiful in this their momentary truth.
The sea mounts the coast,
clings between the rocks, a dazzling spider;
the livid wound on the mountain glistens;
a handful of goats becomes a flock of stones;
the sun lays its gold egg upon the sea.
All is god.
A broken statue,
columns gnawed by the light,
ruins alive in a world of death in life!

Night falls on Teotihuacán.
On top of the pyramid the boys are smoking marijuana,
harsh guitars sound.
What weed, what living waters will give life to us,
where shall we unearth the word,
the relations that govern hymn and speech,
the dance, the city and the measuring scales?
The song of Mexico explodes in a curse,
a coloured star that is extinguished,
a stone that blocks our doors of contact.
Earth tastes of rotten earth.

Eyes see, hands touch.
Here a few things suffice:
prickly pear, coral and thorny planet,
the hooded figs,
grapes that taste of the resurrection,
clams, stubborn maidenheads,
salt, cheese, wine, the sun's bread.
An island girl looks on me from the height of her duskiness,

esbelta catedral vestida de luz.
Torres de sal, contra los pinos verdes de la orilla
surgen las velas blancas de las barcas.
La luz crea templos en el mar.

Nueva York, Londres, Moscú.
La sombra cubre al llano con su yedra fantasma,
con su vacilante vegetación de escalofrío,
su vello ralo, su tropel de ratas.
A trechos tirita un sol anémico.
Acodado en montes que ayer fueron ciudades,
  Polifemo bosteza.
Abajo, entre los hoyos, se arrastra un rebaño de hombres.
Hasta hace poco el vulgo los consideraba animales impuros.

Ver, tocar formas hermosas, diarias.
Zumba la luz, dardos y alas.
Huele a sangre la mancha de vino en el mantel.
Como el coral sus ramas en el agua
extiendo mis sentidos en la hora viva:
el instante se cumple en una concordancia amarilla,
¡oh mediodía, espiga henchida de minutos,
copa de eternidad!

Mis pensamientos se bifurcan, serpean, se enredan,
recomienzan,
y al fin se inmovilizan, ríos que no desembocan,
delta de sangre bajo un sol sin crepúsculo.
¿Y todo ha de parar en este chapoteo de aguas muertas?

¡Día, redondo día,
luminosa naranja de veinticuatro gajos,
todos atravesados por una misma y amarilla dulzura!
La inteligencia al fin encarna,
se reconcilian las dos mitades enemigas
y la conciencia-espejo se licúa,
vuelve a ser fuente, manantial de fábulas:
Hombre, árbol de imágenes,
palabras que son flores que son frutos que son actos.

Nápoles, 1948

a slim cathedral clothed in light.
A tower of salt, against the green pines of the shore,
the white sails of the boats arise.
Light builds temples on the sea.

New York, London, Moscow.
Shadow covers the plain with its phantom ivy,
with its swaying and feverish vegetation,
its mousy fur, its rats' swarm.
Now and then an anaemic sun shivers.
Propping himself on mounts that yesterday were cities,
* Polyphemus yawns.*
Below, among the pits, a herd of men dragging along.
Until lately people considered them unclean animals.

To see, to touch each day's lovely forms.
The light throbs, all arrows and wings.
The wine-stain on the tablecloth smells of blood.
As the coral thrusts branches into the water
I stretch my senses to this living hour:
the moment fulfils itself in a yellow harmony.
Midday, ear of wheat heavy with minutes,
eternity's brimming cup.

My thoughts are split, meander, grow entangled,
start again,
and finally lose headway, endless rivers,
delta of blood beneath an unwinking sun.
And must everything end in this spatter of stagnant water?

Day, round day,
shining orange with four-and-twenty bars,
all one single yellow sweetness!
Mind embodies in forms,
the two hostile become one,
the conscience-mirror liquefies,
once more a fountain of legends:
man, tree of images,
words which are flowers become fruits which are deeds.

[w.c.w.]

El cántaro roto

La mirada interior se despliega y un mundo de vértigo y llama nace bajo
la frente del que sueña:
soles azules, verdes remolinos, picos de luz que abren astros como
granadas,
tornasol solitario, ojo de oro girando en el centro de una explanada
calcinada,
bosques de cristal de sonido, bosques de ecos y respuestas y ondas,
diálogo de transparencias,
¡viento, galope de agua entre los muros interminables de una garganta de
azabache,
caballo, cometa, cohete que se clava justo en el corazón de la noche,
plumas, surtidores,
plumas, súbito florecer de las antorchas, velas, alas, invasión de lo
blanco,
pájaros de las islas cantando bajo la frente del que sueña!

Abrí los ojos, los alcé hasta el cielo y vi cómo la noche se cubría de
estrellas.
¡Islas vivas, brazaletes de islas llameantes, piedras ardiendo, respirando,
racimos de piedras vivas,
cuánta fuente, qué claridades, qué cabelleras sobre una espalda
oscura,
cuanto río allá arriba, y ese sonar remoto del agua junto al fuego, de luz
contra la sombra!
Harpas, jardines de harpas.

Pero a mi lado no había nadie.
Sólo el llano: cactus, huizaches, piedras enormes que estallan bajo el sol.
No cantaba el grillo,
había un vago olor a cal y semillas quemadas,
las calles del poblado eran arroyos secos
y el aire se habría roto en mil pedazos si alguien hubiese gritado: ¿quién
vive?
Cerros pelados, volcán frío, piedra y jadeo bajo tanto esplendor, sequía,
sabor de polvo,
rumor de pies descalzos sobre el polvo, ¡y el pirú en medio del llano
como un surtidor petrificado!

The Broken Waterjar

The inward look unfolds and a world of vertigo and flame is born in the
  dreamer's brow:
blue suns, green whirlwinds, birdbeaks of light pecking open the
  pomegranate stars,
and the solitary sunflower, a gold eye revolving at the centre of a burnt
  slope,
and forests of ringing crystal, forests of echoes and answers and waves,
  a dialogue of transparencies,
and the wind, and the gallop of water between the interminable walls of
  a jet throat,
and the horse, the comet, the skyrocket piercing the night's heart, and
  feathers and fountains,
feathers, a sudden blossoming of torches, candles, wings, an invasion of
  whiteness,
birds of the islands singing in the dreamer's brow!

I opened my eyes, looked up at the sky, and saw how the night was
  covered with stars:
living islands, bracelets of flaming islands, burning and breathing stones,
  clusters of living stones,
and all those fountains and clear lights, those long locks against a dark
  shoulder,
and so many rivers, and the far-off sound of water next to fire, of light
  against shadow!
Harps, gardens of harps.

But I was alone in the field:
it was cactus, and thorns, and great rocks cracking in the sun.
The crickets were silent.
There was a stray odour of lime and burnt seeds,
the village streets were dry gullies,
and the air would have shattered into a thousand pieces if someone had
  shouted: Who goes there?
Bare hills, a cold volcano, stone and a sound of panting under such
  splendour, and drouth, the taste of dust,
the rustle of bare feet in the dust, and one tall tree in the middle of the
  field like a petrified fountain!

Dime, sequía, dime, tierra quemada, tierra de huesos remolidos, dime,
    luna agónica,
¿no hay agua,
hay sólo sangre, sólo hay polvo, sólo pisadas de pies desnudos sobre la
    espina,
sólo andrajos y comida de insectos y sopor bajo el mediodía impío como
    un cacique de oro?
¿No hay relinchos de caballos a la orilla del río, entre las grandes piedras
    redondas y relucientes,
en el remanso, bajo la luz verde de las hojas y los gritos de los hombres y
    las mujeres bañándose al alba?
El dios-maíz, el dios-flor, el dios-agua, el dios-sangre,
    la Virgen,
¿todos se han muerto, se han ido, cántaros rotos al borde de la fuente
    cegada?
¿Sólo está vivo el sapo,
sólo reluce y brilla en la noche de México el sapo verduzco,
sólo el cacique gordo de Cempoala es inmortal?

Tendido al pie divino árbol de jade regado con sangre, mientras dos
    esclavos jóvenes lo abanican,
en los días de las grandes procesiones al frente del pueblo, apoyado en
    la cruz: arma y bastón,
en traje de batalla, el esculpido rostro de sílex aspirando como un incienso
    precioso el humo de los fusilamientos,
los fines de semana en su casa blindada junto al mar, al lado de su querida
    cubierta de joyas de gas neón,
¿sólo el sapo es inmortal?

He aquí a la rabia verde y fría y a su cola de navajas y vidrio cortado,
he aquí al perro y a su aullido sarnoso,
al maguey taciturno, al nopal y al candelabro erizados, he aquí a la flor
    que sangra y hace sangrar,
la flor de inexorable y tajante geometría como un delicado instrumento
    de tortura,
he aquí a la noche de dientes largos y mirada filosa, la noche que desuella
    con un pedernal invisible,
oye a los dientes chocar uno contra otro,
oye a los huesos machacando a los huesos,
al tambor de piel humana golpeado por el fémur,
al tambor del pecho golpeado por el talón rabioso,

Tell me, drouth, tell me, burnt earth, earth of ground bones, tell me,
    agonized moon:
is there no water,
is there only blood, only dust, only naked footsteps on the
    thorns,
only rags and food for insects and stupor under the impious noon, that
    golden chief?
Are there no horses neighing at the riverbank among the great smooth
    glistening boulders,
in the still water, under the green light of the leaves and the shouts of the
    men and women bathing at dawn?
Where are the gods, the corn-god, the flower-god, the water-god, the
    blood-god, the Virgin,
have they all died, have they all departed, broken waterjars at the edge
    of the blocked fount?
Is only the toad alive?
Does only the grey-green toad glow and shine in the Mexican night?
Is only the fat chief of Cempoala immortal?

Reclining under the divine tree of jade which is watered with blood,
    while two young slaves fan him,
leading the great public processions, leaning on the cross: weapon and
    walkingstick,
in battle dress, in a carved stone mask, breathing the smoke of the firing
    squads like a precious incense,
or spending long weekends in his fortified house at the seashore with his
    mistress and her neon jewels?
Is only the toad alive?

Look at the cold green rage with its tail of knives and cut glass,
look at the dog with the mangy howl,
the taciturn maguey, the bristling cactus, the flower that bleeds and lets
    blood,
the flower whose sharp inexorable geometry is like a delicate instrument
    of torture,
look at the night with its long teeth and slashing eyes, the night that
    flays with an invisible stone,
listen to the teeth colliding,
listen to the bones crushing bones,
the thighbone pounding the drum of human skin,
the furious heel pounding the drum of the breast,

27

al tam-tam de los tímpanos golpeados por el sol delirante,
he aquí al polvo que se levanta como un rey amarillo y todo lo descuaja
   y danza solitario y se derrumba
como un árbol al que de pronto se la han secado las raíces, como una
   torre que cae de un solo tajo,
he aquí al hombre que cae y se levanta y come polvo y se arrastra,
al insecto humano que perfora la piedra y perfora los sigleos y carcome la
   luz,
he aquí a la piedra rota, al hombre roto, a la luz rota.

¿Abrir los ojos o cerrarlos, todo es igual?
Castillos interiores que incendia el pensamiento porque otro más puro
   se levante, sólo fulgor y llama,
semilla de la imagen que crece hasta ser árbol y hace estallar el cráneo,
palabra que busca unos labios que la digan,
sobre la antigua fuente humana cayeron grandes piedras,
hay siglos de piedras, años de losas, minutos espesores sobre la fuente
   humana.

Dime, sequía, piedra pulida por el tiempo sin dientes, por el hambre sin
   dientes,
polvo molido por dientes que son siglos, por siglos que
   son hambres,
dime, cántaro roto caído en el polvo, dime,
¿la luz nace frotando hueso contra hueso, hombre contra hombre,
   hambre, contra hambre,
hasta que surja al fin la chispa, el grito, la palabra,
hasta que brote al fin el agua y crezca el árbol de anchas hojas de
   turquesa?

Hay que dormir con los ojos abiertos, hay que soñar con las manos,
soñemos sueños activos de río buscando su cauce, sueños de sol soñando
   sus mundos,
hay que soñar en voz alta, hay que cantar hasta que el canto eche raíces,
   tronco, ramas, pájaros, astros,
cantar hasta que el sueño engendre y brote del costado del dormido la
   espiga roja de la resurrección,
el agua de la mujer, el manantial para beber y mirarse y reconocerse y
   recobrarse,
el manantial para saberse hombre, el agua que habla a solas en la noche y
   nos llama con nuestro nombre,

the delirious sun pounding the tom-tom of the eardrums,
look at the dust that rises like a yellow king and uproots everything and
   dances alone and falls down
like a tree whose roots have suddenly dried up, like a tower collapsing at
   the first blow,
look at the man who falls and rises and eats dust and crawls along,
the human insect who pierces the rock and pierces the centuries and
   gnashes at the light,
look at the broken rock, the broken man, the broken light.

Is it all the same if we open our eyes or close them?
Thought burns down our interior castles so that another may rise in
   their place, all flame and refulgence,
the seed of an image growing up into a tree that cracks the skull,
the word seeking lips that will speak it.
Great stones have cumbered the ancient human fount,
there are centuries of stones, years of flagstones, ponderous stone
   minutes heaped over the human fount.

Tell me, drouth, stone polished smooth by toothless time, by toothless
   hunger,
dust ground to dust by teeth that are centuries, by centuries that are
   hunger,
tell me, broken waterjar in the dust, tell me,
is the light born to rub bone against bone, man against man, hunger
   against hunger,
till the spark, the cry, the word spurts forth at last,
till the water flows and the tree with wide turquoise leaves arises at
   last?

We must sleep with open eyes, we must dream with our hands,
we must dream the dreams of a river seeking its course, of the sun
   dreaming its worlds,
we must dream aloud, we must sing till the song puts forth roots, trunk,
   branches, birds, stars,
we must sing till the dream engenders in the sleeper's flank the red
   wheat-ear of resurrection,
the womanly water, the spring at which we may drink and recognize
   ourselves and recover,
the spring that tells us we are men, the water that speaks alone in the
   night and calls us by name,

el manantial de las palabras para decir yo, tú, él, nosotros, bajo el gran
árbol viviente estatua de la lluvia,
para decir los pronombres hermosos y reconocernos y ser fieles a
nuestros nombres
hay que soñar hacia atrás, hacia la fuente, hay que remar siglos arriba,
más allá de la infancia, más allá del comienzo, más allá de las aguas del
bautismo,
echar abajo las paredes entre el hombre y el hombre, juntar de nuevo lo
que fue separado,
vida y muerte no son mundos contrarios, somos un solo tallo con dos
flores gemelas,
hay que desenterrar la palabra perdida, soñar hacia dentro y también
hacia afuera,
descifrar el tatuaje de la noche y mirar cara a cara al mediodía y arrancarle
su máscara,
bañarse en luz solar y comer los frutos nocturnos, deletrear la escritura
del astro y la del río,
recordar lo que dicen la sangre y la marea, la tierra y el cuerpo, volver al
punto de partida,
ni adentro ni afuera, ni arriba ni abajo, al cruce de caminos, adonde
empiezan los caminos,
porque la luz canta con un rumor de agua, con un rumor de follaje
canta el agua
y el alba está cargada de frutos, el día y la noche reconciliados fluyen
como un río manso,
el día y la noche se acarician largamente como un hombre y una mujer
enamorados,
como un solo río interminable bajo arcos de siglos fluyen las estaciones y
los hombres,
hacia allá, al centro vivo del origen, más allá de fin y comienzo.

México, 1955

the spring of words that say I, you, he, we, under the great tree, the
living statue of the rain,
where we pronounce the beautiful pronouns, knowing ourselves and
keeping faith with our names,
we must dream backwards, toward the source, we must row back up the
centuries,
beyond infancy, beyond the beginning, beyond the waters of baptism,
we must break down the walls between man and man, reunite what has
been sundered,
life and death are not opposite worlds, we are one stem with twin
flowers,
we must find the lost word, dream inwardly and also
outwardly,
decipher the night's tattooing and look face to face at the noonday and
tear off its mask,
bathe in the light of the sun and eat the night's fruit and spell out the
writings of stars and rivers,
and remember what the blood, the tides, the earth, and the body say,
and return to the point of departure,
neither inside nor outside, neither up nor down, at the crossroads where
all roads begin,
for the light is singing with a sound of water, the water with a sound of
leaves,
the dawn is heavy with fruit, the day and the night flow together in
reconciliation like a calm river,
the day and the night caress each other like a man and woman in
love,
and the seasons and all mankind are flowing under the arches of the
centuries like one endless river
toward the living centre of origin, beyond the end and the beginning.

[L.K.]

El río

La ciudad desvelada circula por mi sangre como una abeja.
Y el avión que traza un gemido en forma de S larga, los tranvías que se
    derrumban en esquinas remotas,
ese árbol cargado de injurias que alguien sacude a medianoche en la
    plaza,
los ruidos que ascienden y estallan y los que se deslizan y cuchichean en
    la oreja un secreto que repta
abren lo oscuro, precipicios de aes y oes, túneles de vocales
    taciturnas,
galerías que recorro con los ojos vendados, el alfabeto somnoliento cae
    en el hoyo como un río de tinta,
y la ciudad va y viene y su cuerpo de piedra se hace añicos al llegar a mi
    sien,
toda la noche, uno a uno, estatua a estatua, fuente a fuente, piedra a piedra,
    toda la noche
sus pedazos se buscan en mi frente, toda la noche la ciudad habla dormida
    por mi boca
y es un discurso y jadeante, un tartamudeo de aguas y piedra batallando,
    su historia.

Detenerse un instante, detener a mi sangre que va y viene, va y viene y
    no dice nada,
sentado sobre mí mismo como el yoguín a la sombra de la higuera, como
    Buda a la orilla del río, detener al instante,
un solo instante, sentado a la orilla del tiempo, borrar mi imagen del río
    que habla dormido y no dice nada y me lleva consigo,
sentado a la orilla detener al río, abrir el instante, penetrar por sus salas
    atónitas hasta su centro de agua,
beber en la fuente, ser la cascada de sílabas azules que cae de los labios de
    piedra,
sentado a la orilla de la noche como Buda a la orilla de sí mismo ser el
    parpadeo del instante,
el incendio y la destrucción y el nacimiento del instante y la respiración
    de la noche fluyendo enorme a la orilla del tiempo,
decir lo que dice el río, larga palabra semejante a labios, larga palabra que
    no acaba nunca,
decir lo que dice el tiempo en duras frases de piedra, en vastos ademanes
    de mar cubriendo mundos.

The River

The restless city circles in my blood like a bee.
And the plane that traces a querulous moan in a long ´S, the trams that
break down on remote corners,
that tree weighted with affronts that someone shakes at midnight in the
plaza,
the noises that rise and shatter and those that fade away and whisper a
secret that wriggles in the ear,
they open the darkness, precipices of a's and o's, tunnels of taciturn
vowels,
galleries I run down blindfolded, the drowsy alphabet falls in the pit like
a river of ink,
and the city goes and comes and its stone body shatters as it arrives at
my temple,
all night, one by one, statue by statue, fountain by fountain, stone by
stone, the whole night long
its shards seek one another in my forehead, all night long the city talks
in its sleep through my mouth,
a gasping discourse, a stammering of waters and arguing stone, its
story.

To stop still an instant, to still my blood which goes and comes, goes and
comes and says nothing,
seated on top of me like a yogi in the shadow of a fig tree, like Buddha
on the river's edge, to stop the instant,
a single instant, seated on the edge of time, to strike out my image of the
river that talks in its sleep and says nothing and carries me with it,
seated on the bank to stop the river, to unlock the instant, to penetrate its
astonished rooms reaching the centre of water,
to drink at the fountain, to be the cascade of blue syllables falling from
stone lips,
seated on the edge of night like Buddha on his self's edge, to be the
flicker of the lidded instant,
the conflagration and the destruction and the birth of the instant, the
breathing of night rushing enormous at the edge of time,
to say what the river says, a long word resembling lips, a long word that
never ends,
to say what time says in hard sentences of stone, in vast gestures of sea
covering worlds.

A mitad del poema me sobrecoge siempre un gran desamparo, todo me
abandona,
no hay nadie a mi lado, ni siquiera esos ojos que desde atrás contemplan
lo que escribo,
no hay atrás ni adelante, la pluma se rebela, no hay comienzo ni fin,
tampoco hay muro que saltar,
es una explanada desierta el poema, lo dicho no está dicho, lo no dicho es
indecible,
torres, terrazas devastadas, babilonias, un mar de sal negra, un reino
ciego,
        No,
detenerme, callar, cerrar los ojos hasta que brote de mis párpados una
espiga, un surtidor de soles,
y el alfabeto ondule largamente bajo el viento del sueño y la marea
crezca en una ola y la ola rompa el dique,
esperar hasta que el papel se cubra de astros y sea el poema un bosque de
palabras enlazadas,
        No,
no tengo nada que decir, nadie tiene nada que decir, nada ni nadie
excepto la sangre,
nada sino este ir y venir de la sangre, este escribir sobre lo escrito y
repetir la misma palabra en mitad del poema,
sílabas de tiempo, letras rotas, gotas de tinta, sangre que va y viene y no
dice nada y me lleva consigo.

Y digo mi rostro inclinado sobre el papel y alguien a mi lado escribe
mientras la sangre va y viene,
y la ciudad va y viene por su sangre, quiere decir algo, el tiempo quiere
decir algo, la noche quiere decir,
toda la noche el hombre quiere decir una sola palabra, decir al fin su
discurso hecho de piedras desmoronadas,
y aguzo el oído, quiero oír lo que dice el hombre, repetir lo que dice la
ciudad a la deriva,
toda la noche las piedras rotas se buscan a tientas en mi frente, toda la
noche pelea el agua contra la piedra,
las palabras contra la noche, la noche contra la noche, nada ilumina el
opaco combate,
el choque de las armas no arranca un relámpago a la piedra, una chispa a
la noche, nadie da tregua,
es un combate a muerte entre inmortales dar marcha atrás, parar el río
de sangre, el río de tinta,

In mid-poem a great helplessness overtakes me, everything abandons me,

there is no one beside me, not even those eyes that gaze from behind me at what I write,

no one behind or in front of me, the pen mutinies, there is neither beginning nor end nor even a wall to leap,

the poem is a deserted esplanade, what's said is not said, the unsaid is unsayable,

towers, devastated terraces, Babylons, a sea of black salt, a blind kingdom,

No,

to stop myself, to keep quiet, to close my eyes until a green spike sprouts. from my eyelids, a spurt of suns,

and the alphabet wavers long under the wind of the vision and the tide rolls into one wave and the wave breaks the dike,

to wait until the paper is covered with stars and the poem a forest of tangled words,

No,

I have nothing to say, no one has anything to say, nothing and nobody except the blood,

nothing except this coming and going of the blood, this writing over the written, the repetition of the same word in mid-poem,

syllables of time, broken letters, splotches of ink, blood that goes and comes and says nothing and carries me with it.

And I speak, my face bent over the paper and someone beside me writes while the blood goes and comes,

and the city goes and comes through his blood, wants to say something, time wants to say something, the night wants to speak,

all night long the man wants to say one single word, to speak his discourse at last, made up of mouldered stones,

and I whet my hearing, I want to hear what the man says, to repeat what the drifting city says,

all night the broken stones seek one another, groping in my forehead, all night the water fights the stone,

the words against the night, the night against the night, nothing lights up the opaque combat,

the shock of arms does not wrench away a single gleam to the stone, one spark to the night, no one grants a respite,

it is a fight to the death between immortals to offer retreat, to stop the river of blood, the river of ink,

parar el río de las palabras, remontar la corriente y que la noche vuelta
sobre sí misma muestre sus entrañas de oro ardiendo,
que el agua muestre su corazón que es un racimo de espejos ahogados,
un árbol de cristal que el viento desarraiga
(y cada hoja del árbol vuela y centellea y se pierde en una luz cruel
como se pierden las palabras en la imagen del poeta)
que el tiempo se cierre y sea su herida una cicatriz invisible, apenas una
delgada línea sobre la piel del mundo,
que las palabras depongan armas y sea el poema una sola palabra entrete-
jida, un resplandor implacable que avanza,
y sea el alma el llano después del incendio, el pecho lunar de un mar
petrificado que no refleja nada
sino la extensión extendida, el espacio acostado sobre sí mismo, las alas
inmensas desplegadas,
y sea todo como la llama que se esculpe y se hiela en la roca de entrañas
transparentes,
duro fulgor resuelto ya en cristal y claridad pacífica.

Y el río remonta su curso, repliega sus velas, recoge sus imágenes y se
interna en sí mismo.

Ginebra, 1953

to stop the river of words, to go back upstream, and that the night turn
upon itself display its bowels of flaming gold,
and that the water show its heart, a cluster of drowned mirrors, a glass
tree that the wind uproots
(and every leaf of the tree flutters and glints and is lost in a cruel light,
as the words of the poet's image are lost),
may time thicken and its wound be an invisible scar, scarcely a delicate
line upon the skin of the world,
let the words lay down their arms and the poem be one single interwoven
word, an implacable radiance that advances
and may the soul be the blackened grass after fire, the lunar breast of a
sea that's turned to stone and reflects nothing
except splayed dimension, expansion, space lying down upon itself,
spread wings immense,
and may everything be like flame that cuts itself into and freezes into the
rock of diaphanous bowels,
hard blazing resolved now in crystal, peaceable clarity.

And the river goes back upstream, strikes its sails, picks up its images and
coils within itself.

[P.B.]

from *¿Aguila o sol?* (1949–50)

from *Trabajos del poeta*

VII

Escribo sobre la mesa crepuscular, apoyando fuerte la pluma sobre su pecho casi vivo, que gime y recuerda al bosque natal. La tinta negra abre sus grandes alas. La lámpara estalla y cubre mis palabras una capa de cristales rotos. Un fragmento afilado de luz me corta la mano derecha. Continúo escribiendo con ese muñón que mana sombra. La noche entra en el cuarto, el muro de enfrente adelanta su jeta de piedra, grandes témpanos de aire se interponen entre la pluma y el papel. Un simple monosílabo bastaría para hacer saltar al mundo. Pero esta noche no hay sitio para una sola palabra más.

XIII

Hace años, con piedrecitas, basuras y yerbas, edifiqué Tilantlán. Recuerdo la muralla, las puertas amarillas con el signo digital, las calles estrechas y malolientes que habitaba una plebe ruidosa, el verde Palacio del Gobierno y la roja Casa de los Sacrificios, abierta como una mano, con sus cinco grandes templos y sus calzadas innumerables. Tilantlán, ciudad gris al pie de la piedra blanca, ciudad agarrada al suelo con uñas y dientes, ciudad de polvo y plegarias. Sus moradores – astutos, ceremoniosos y coléricos – adoraban a las Manos, que los habían hecho, pero temían a los Pies, que podrían destruirlos. Su teología, y los renovados sacrificios con que intentaron comprar el amor de las Primeras y asegurarse la benevolencia de los Últimos, no evitaron que una alegre mañana mi pie derecho los aplastara, con su historia, su aristocracia feroz, sus motines, su lenguaje sagrado, sus canciones populares y su teatro ritual. Y sus sacerdotes jamás sospecharon que Pies y Manos no eran sino las extremidades de un mismo dios.

from *The Poet's Works*

VII

I write on the crepuscular table, my pen resting heavily on its chest that is almost living, that moans and remembers the forest of its birth. Great wings of black ink open. The lamp explodes and a cape of broken glass covers my words. A sharp sliver of light cuts off my right hand. I keep writing with this stump that sprouts shadows. Night enters the room, the opposite wall puckers its big stone lips, great blocks of air come between my pen and the paper. A simple monosyllable would be enough to blow up the world! But tonight there is no room for a single word more.

XIII

Years ago, out of pebbles, garbage and grass, I built Tilantlán. I remember the wall, the yellow doors with the digital sign, the narrow, stinking streets inhabited by a noisy populace, the green Government Palace, and the red House of the Sacrifices, open like a hand, with its five great temples and its countless causeways. Tilantlán, grey city at the foot of the white rock, city gripped to the ground by nails and teeth, city of dust and prayers. Its inhabitants – astute, ceremonious and passionate – worshipped the Hands that had made them, but feared the Feet that could destroy them. Their theology, and the fresh sacrifices with which they intended to buy the love of the Firsts and insure the benevolence of the Lasts, did not spare them that happy morning when my right foot crushed them and their history, their fierce aristocracy, their insurrections, their sacred language, their folksongs and ritual theatre. Their priests never suspected that Feet and Hands were but extremities of the same god.

XIV

Difícilmente, avanzando milímetros por año, me hago un camino entre
la roca. Desde hace milenios mis dientes se gastan y mis uñas se rompen
para llegar allá, al otro lado, a la luz y el aire libre. Y ahora que mis
manos sangran y mis dientes tiemblan, inseguros, en una cavidad rajada
por la sed y es polvo, me detengo y contemplo mi obra: he pasado la
segunda parte de mi vida rompiendo las piedras, perforando las murallas,
taladrando las puertas y apartando los obstáculos que interpuse entre la
luz y yo durante la primera parte de mi vida.

XVI

Como un dolor que avanza y se abre paso entre vísceras que ceden y
huesos que resisten, como una lima que lima los nervios que nos atan a la
vida, sí, pero también como una alegría súbita, como abrir una puerta
que da al mar, como asomarse al abismo y como llegar a la cumbre,
como el río de diamante que horada la roca y como la cascada azul que
cae en un derrumbe de estatuas y templos blanquísimos, como el pájaro
que sube y el relámpago que desciende, ¡oh batir de alas, oh pico que
desgarra y entreabre al fin el fruto!, tú, mi grito, surtidor de plumas de
fuego, herida resonante y vasta como el desprendimiento de un planeta
del cuerpo de una estrella, caída infinita en un cielo de ecos, en un cielo
de espejos que te repiten y destrozan y te vuelven innumerable, infinito
y anónimo.

XIV

With great difficulty, advancing by millimetres each year, I carve a road
out of the rock. For millennia my teeth have wasted and my nails broken
to get *there*, to the other side, to the light and the open air. And now that
my hands bleed and my teeth tremble, unsure, in a cavity cracked by
thirst and dust, I pause and contemplate my work: I have spent the
second part of my life breaking the stones, drilling the walls, smashing
the doors and removing the obstacles I placed between the light and
myself in the first part of my life.

XVI

Like a pain that moves forward opening a passage between the yielding
guts and the resisting bones, like a file that files the nerves that tie us to
life, yes, but also like a sudden joy, like opening a door that fronts the
sea, like looking down into the abyss, like reaching the summit, like the
diamond river that wears away the rock and like the blue cascade that
falls in a landslide of statues and white temples, like the bird that rises
and the lightning that falls, flash of wings, beak that tears and at last
cracks open the fruit! You my cry, fountain of feathers of fire, wound
resounding and vast like the ripping out of a planet from the body of a
star, infinitely falling in a sky of echoes, in a sky of mirrors that repeat
you and destroy and restore you innumerable, infinite, anonymous.

[E.W.]

from *Arenas movedizas*

El ramo azul

Desperté, cubierto de sudor. Del piso de ladrillos rojos, recién regado, subía un vapor caliente. Una mariposa de alas grisáceas revoloteaba encandilada alrededor del foco amarillento. Salté de la hamaca y descalzo atravesé el cuarto, cuidando no pisar algún alacrán salido de su escondrijo a tomar el fresco. Me acerqué al ventanillo y aspiré el aire del campo. Se oía la respiración de la noche, enorme, femenina. Regresé al centro de la habitación, vacié el agua de la jarra en la palangana de peltre y humedecí la toalla. Me froté el torso y las piernas con el trapo empapado, me sequé un poco y, tras de cerciorarme que ningún bicho estaba escondido entre los pliegues de mi ropa, me vestí y calcé. Bajé saltando la escalera pintada de verde. En la puerta del mesón tropecé con el dueño, sujeto tuerto y reticente. Sentado en una sillita de tule, fumaba con el ojo entrecerrado. Con voz ronca me preguntó:

– ¿Ónde va, señor?

– A dar una vuelta. Hace mucho calor.

– Hum, todo está ya cerrado. Y no hay alumbrado aquí. Más le valiera quedarse.

Alcé los hombros, musité 'ahora vuelvo' y me metí en lo oscuro. Al principio no veía nada. Caminé a tientas por la calle empedrada. Encendí un cigarrillo. De pronto salió la luna de una nube negra, iluminando un muro blanco, desmoronado a trechos. Me detuve, ciego ante tanta blancura. Sopló un poco de viento. Respiré el aire de los tamarindos. Vibraba la noche, llena de hojas e insectos. Los grillos vivaqueaban entre las hierbas altas. Alcé la cara: arriba también habían establecido campamento las estrellas. Pensé que el universo era un vasto sistema de señales, una conversación entre seres inmensos. Mis actos, el serrucho del grillo, el parpadeo de la estrella, no eran sino pausas y sílabas, frases dispersas de aquel diálogo. ¿Cuál sería esa palabra de la cual yo era una sílaba? ¿Quién dice esa palabra y a quién se la dice? Tiré el cigarrillo sobre la banqueta. Al caer, describió una curva luminosa, arrojando breves chispas, como un cometa minúsculo.

Caminé largo rato, despacio. Me sentía libre, seguro entre los labios que en ese momento me pronunciaban con tanta felicidad. La noche

from *Shifting Sands*

The Blue Bouquet

I woke covered with sweat. Hot steam rose from the newly-sprayed, red brick pavement. A grey-winged butterfly, dazzled, circled the yellow light. I jumped from my hammock and crossed the room barefoot, careful not to step on some scorpion leaving his hideout for a bit of fresh air. I went to the little window and inhaled the country air. One could hear the breathing of the night, feminine, enormous. I returned to the centre of the room, emptied water from a jar into a pewter basin, and wet my towel. I rubbed my chest and legs with the soaked cloth, dried myself a little, and, making sure that no bugs were hidden in the folds of my clothes, got dressed. I ran down the green stairway. At the door of the boarding house I bumped into the owner, a one-eyed, taciturn fellow. Sitting on a wicker stool, he smoked, his eye half-closed. In a hoarse voice, he asked:

'Where you going?'

'To take a walk. It's too hot.'

'Hmmm – everything's closed. And no streetlights around here. You'd better stay put.'

I shrugged my shoulders, muttered 'back soon', and plunged into the darkness. At first I couldn't see anything. I fumbled along the cobblestone street. I lit a cigarette. Suddenly the moon appeared from behind a black cloud, lighting a white wall that was crumbled in places. I stopped, blinded by such whiteness. Wind whistled slightly. I breathed the air of the tamarinds. The night hummed, full of leaves and insects. Crickets bivouacked in the tall grass. I raised my head: up there the stars too had set up camp. I thought that the universe was a vast system of signs, a conversation between giant beings. My actions, the cricket's saw, the star's blink, were nothing but pauses and syllables, scattered phrases from that dialogue. What word could it be, of which I was only a syllable? Who speaks the word? To whom is it spoken? I threw my cigarette down on the sidewalk. Falling, it drew a shining curve, shooting out brief sparks like a tiny comet.

I walked a long time, slowly. I felt free, secure between the lips that were at that moment speaking me with such happiness. The night was a

era un jardín de ojos. Al cruzar una calle, sentí que alguien se desprendía de una puerta. Me volví, pero no acerté a distinguir nada. Apreté el paso. Unos instantes después percibí el apagado rumor de unos huaraches sobre las piedras calientes. No quise volverme, aunque sentía que la sombra se acercaba cada vez más. Intenté correr. No pude. Me detuve en seco, bruscamente. Antes de que pudiese defenderme, sentí la punta de un cuchillo en mi espalda y una voz dulce:

– No se mueva, señor, o se lo entierro.

Sin volver la cara, pregunté:

– ¿Qué quieres?

– Sus ojos, señor – contestó la voz suave, casi apenada.

– ¿Mis ojos? ¿Para qué te servirán mis ojos? Mira, aquí tengo un poco de dinero. No es mucho, pero es algo. Te daré todo lo que tengo, si me dejas. No vayas a matarme.

– No tenga miedo, señor. No lo mataré. Nada más voy a sacarle los ojos.

Volví a preguntar:

– Pero, ¿para qué quieres mis ojos?

– Es un capricho de mi novia. Quiere un ramito de ojos azules. Y por aquí hay pocos que los tengan.

– Mis ojos no te sirven. No son azules, sino amarillos.

– Ay, señor, no quiera engañarme. Bien sé que los tiene azules.

– No se le sacan a un cristiano los ojos así. Te daré otra cosa.

– No se haga el remilgoso, me dijo con dureza. Dé la vuelta.

Me volví. Era pequeño y frágil. El sombrero de palma le cubría medio rostro. Sostenía con el brazo derecho un machete de campo, que brillaba con la luz de la luna.

– Alúmbrese la cara.

Encendí y me acerqué la llama al rostro. El resplandor me hizo entrecerrar los ojos. Él apartó mis párpados con mano firme. No podía ver bien. Se alzó sobre las puntas de los pies y me contempló intensamente. La llama me quemaba los dedos. La arrojé. Permaneció un instante silencioso.

– ¿Ya te convenciste? No los tengo azules.

– Ah, qué mañoso es usted – respondió –. A ver, encienda otra vez.

Froté otro fósforo y lo acerqué a mis ojos. Tirándome de la manga, me ordenó:

– Arrodíllese.

Me hinqué. Con una mano me cogió por los cabellos, echándome la cabeza hacia atrás. Se inclinó sobre mí, curioso y tenso, mientras el machete descendía lentamente hasta rozar mis párpados. Cerré los ojos.

garden of eyes. As I crossed the street, I heard someone come out of a doorway. I turned around, but could not distinguish anything. I hurried on. A few moments later I heard the dull shuffle of sandals on the hot stone. I didn't want to turn around, although I felt the shadow getting closer with every step. I tried to run. I couldn't. Suddenly I stopped short. Before I could defend myself, I felt the point of a knife in my back, and a sweet voice:

'Don't move, mister, or I'll stick it in.'

Without turning, I asked:

'What do you want?'

'Your eyes, mister,' answered the soft, almost painful voice.

'My eyes? What do you want with my eyes? Look, I've got some money. Not much, but it's something. I'll give you everything I have if you let me go. Don't kill me.'

'Don't be afraid, mister. I won't kill you. I'm only going to take your eyes.'

'But why do you want my eyes?' I asked again.

'My girlfriend has this whim. She wants a bouquet of blue eyes. And around here they're hard to find.'

'My eyes won't help you. They're brown, not blue.

'Don't try to fool me, mister. I know very well that yours are blue.'

'Don't take the eyes of a fellow man. I'll give you something else.'

'Don't play saint with me,' he said harshly. 'Turn around.'

I turned. He was small and fragile. His palm sombrero covered half his face. In his right hand he held a country machete that shone in the moonlight.

'Let me see your face.'

I struck a match and put it close to my face. The brightness made me squint. He opened my eyelids with a firm hand. He couldn't see very well. Standing on tip-toe, he stared at me intensely. The flame burned my fingers. I dropped it. A silent moment passed.

'Are you convinced now? They're not blue.'

'Pretty clever, aren't you?' he answered. 'Let's see. Light another one.'

I struck another match, and put it near my eyes. Grabbing my sleeve, he ordered:

'Kneel down.'

I knelt. With one hand he grabbed me by the hair, pulling my head back. He bent over me, curious and tense, while his machete slowly dropped until it grazed my eyelids. I closed my eyes.

– Ábralos bien – ordenó.
Abrí los ojos. La llamita me quemaba las pestañas. Me soltó de improviso.
– Pues no son azules, señor. Dispense.
Y desapareció. Me acodé junto al muro, con la cabeza entre las manos. Luego me incorporé. A tropezones, cayendo y levantándome, corrí durante una hora por el pueblo desierto. Cuando llegué a la plaza, vi al dueño del mesón, sentado aún frente a la puerta. Entré sin decir palabra. Al día siguiente huí de aquel pueblo.

'Keep them open,' he ordered.

I opened my eyes. The flame burned my lashes. All of a sudden, he let me go.

'All right, they're not blue. Beat it.'

He vanished. I leaned against the wall, my head in my hands. I pulled myself together. Stumbling, falling, trying to get up again, I ran for an hour through the deserted town. When I got to the plaza, I saw the owner of the boarding house, still sitting in front of the door. I went in without saying a word. The next day I left town.

[E.W.]

from *¿Aguila o sol?*

Jardín con niño

A tientas, me adentro. Pasillos, puertas que dan a un cuarto de hotel, a una interjección, a un páramo urbano. Y entre el bostezo y el abandono, tú, intacto, verdor sitiado por tanta muerte, jardín revisto esta noche. Sueños insensatos y lúcidos, geometría y delirio entre altas bardas de adobe. La glorieta de los pinos, ocho testigos de mi infancia, siempre de pie, sin cambiar nunca de postura, de traje, de silencio. El montón de pedruscos de aquel pabellón que no dejó terminar la guerra civil, lugar amado por la melancolía y las lagartijas. Los yerbales, con sus secretos, su molicie de verde caliente, sus bichos agazapados y terribles. La higuera y sus consejas. Los adversarios: el floripondio y sus lámparas blancas frente al granado, candelabro de joyas rojas ardiendo en pleno día. El membrillo y sus varas flexibles, con las que arrancaba ayes al aire matinal. La lujosa mancha de vino de la bugambilia sobre el muro inmaculado, blanquísimo. El sitio sagrado, el lugar infame, el rincón del monólogo: la orfandad de una tarde, los himnos de una mañana, los silencios, aquel día de gloria entrevista, compartida.

Arriba, en la espesura de las ramas, entre los claros del cielo y las encrucijadas de los verdes, la tarde se bate son espadas transparentes. Piso la tierra recién llovida, los olores ásperos, las yerbas vivas. El silencio se yergue y me interroga. Pero yo avanzo y me planto en el centro de mi memoria. Aspiro largamente el aire cargado de porvenir. Vienen oleadas de futuro, rumor de conquistas, descubrimientos y esos vacíos súbitos con que prepara lo desconocido sus irrupciones. Silbo entre dientes y mi silbido, en la limpidez admirable de la hora, es un látigo alegre que despierta alas y echa a volar profecías. Y yo las veo partir hacia allá, al otro lado, a donde un hombre encorvado escribe trabajosamente, en camisa, entre pausas furiosas, estos cuantos adioses al borde del precipicio.

from *Eagle or Sun?*

Garden and Child

Uncertainly, I enter. Corridors, doors that open on a hotel room, on an interjection, on an urban desert. And between yawn and desertion, you, intact, foliage besieged by so much death, garden seen again tonight. Senseless and lucid dreams, geometry and delirium between high walls of adobe. The arbour of pines, eight witnesses to my childhood, always standing, never changing their posture, their dress, their silence. The pile of stones for the pavilion that the civil war kept unfinished, a place loved by melancholy and the lizards. The tall grasses with their secrets, their hot green softness, their crouching, terrifying bugs. The fig tree with its fables. The enemies: the magnolia with its white lamps in front of the pomegranate tree, candelabra of red jewels burning in the full sun. The quince and its elastic branches that drew sighs from the morning air. The rich wine-stain of the bougainvillea on the immaculate, so very white, wall. The sacred place, the infamous site, the corner of the monologue: the orphanage of an afternoon, the hymns of a morning, the silences, that day of a paradise glimpsed and shared.

Above, in the thickness of the branches, between the gaps of sky and the crossroads of green, the afternoon battles with transparent swords. I step on newly rained earth, the smells sharp, the grass vivid. Silence stands erect and questions me. But I move forward, and plant myself in the centre of my memory. I breathe deeply this air charged with things to come. Swells of the future approach, rumours of conquests, discoveries and those sudden voids with which the unknown prepares its invasions. I whistle between my teeth, and my whistle, in the admirable clarity of the hour, is a happy whiplash that wakens wings and starts prophecies flying. And I watch them leave for *there*, for the other side, where a hunched man in shirtsleeves laboriously writes, between furious pauses, those few goodbyes from the brink of the precipice.

[E.W.]

Llano

El hormiguero hace erupción. La herida abierta borbotea, espumea, se expande, se contrae. El sol a estas horas no deja nunca de bombear sangre, con las sienes hinchadas, la cara roja. Un niño – ignorante de que en un recodo de la pubertad lo esperan unas fiebres y un problema de conciencia – coloca con cuidado una piedrecita en la boca despellejada del hormiguero. El sol hunde sus picas en las jorobas del llano, humilla promontorios de basura. Resplandor desenvainado, los reflejos de una lata vacía – erguida sobre una pirámide de piltrafas – acuchillan todos los puntos del espacio. Los niños buscadores de tesoros y los perros sin dueño escarban en el amarillo esplendor del pudridero. A trescientos metros la iglesia de San Lorenzo llama a misa de doce. Adentro, en el altar de la derecha, hay un santo pintado de azul y rosa. De su ojo izquierdo brota un enjambre de insectos de alas grises, que vuelan en línea recta hacia la cúpula y caen, hechos polvo, silencioso derrumbe de armaduras tocadas por la mano del sol. Silban las sirenas de las torres de las fábricas. Falos decapitados. Un pájaro vestido de negro vuela en círculos y se posa en el único árbol vivo del llano. Después ... No hay después. Avanzo, perforo grandes rocas de años, grandes masas de luz compacta, desciendo galerías de minas de arena, atravieso corredores que se cierran como labios de granito. Y vuelvo al llano, al llano donde siempre es mediodía, donde un sol idéntico cae fijamente sobre un paisaje detenido. Y no acaban de caer las doce campanadas, ni de zumbar las moscas, ni de estallar en astillas este minuto que no pasa, que sólo arde y no pasa.

Nota arriesgada

Templada nota que avanzas por un país de nieve y alas, entre despeñaderos y picos donde afilan su navaja los astros, acompañada sólo por un murmullo grave de cola aterciopelada, ¿adónde te diriges? Pájaro negro, tu pico hace saltar las rocas. Tu imperio enlutado vuelve ilusorios los precarios límites entre el hierro y el girasol, la piedra y el ave, el fuego y el liquen. Arrancas a la altura réplicas ardientes. La luz de cuello de vidrio se parte en dos y tu negra armadura se constela de frialdades intactas. Ya estás entre las transparencias y tu penacho blanco ondea en

Plain

The anthill erupts. The open wound gushes, foams, expands, contracts. The sun at these times never stops pumping blood, temples swollen, face red. A boy – unaware that, in some corner of puberty, fevers and a problem of conscience await him – carefully places a small stone on the flayed mouth of the anthill. The sun buries its lances in the humps of the plain, crushing promontories of garbage. Splendour unsheathed, the reflections from an empty can – high on a pyramid of scraps – pierce every point of space. Treasure-hunting children and stray dogs poke in the yellow radiance of the rot. A thousand feet away, the church of San Lorenzo calls the twelve o'clock mass. Inside, on the altar to the right, there is a saint painted blue and pink. From his left eye stream grey-winged insects that fly in a straight line to the dome and fall turned to dust, a silent landslide of armour touched by the sun's hand. Whistles blow in the towers of the factories. Decapitated phalluses. A bird, dressed in black, flies in circles and rests on the only living tree on the plain. And then . . . There is no then. I move forward, I pierce great rocks of years, great masses of compacted light, I go down into galleries of mines of sand, I travel corridors that close on themselves like granite lips. And I return to the plain, to the plain where it is always noon, where an identical sun shines fixedly on an unmoving landscape. And the ringing of the twelve bells never stops, nor the buzzing of the flies, nor the explosion of this minute that never passes, that only burns and never passes.

[E.W.]

Daring Note

Brave note you advance through a country of snow and wings, between precipices and peaks where the stars sharpen their razors, accompanied only by the heavy murmur of your velvety tail – where are you going? Black bird, your beak explodes the rocks. Your veiled kingdom renders illusory the precarious line between iron and sunflower, rock and bird, fire and lichen. You tear burning answers from the heights. The light with its glass necks splits in two, and your black armour sparkles of pure cold. You are already among the transparencies and your white crest

mil sitios a la vez, cisne ahogado en su propia blancura. Te posas en la cima y clavas tu centella. Después, inclinándote, besas los labios congelados del cráter. Es hora de estallar en una explosión que no dejará más huella que una larga cicatriz en el cielo. Cruzas los corredores de la música y desapareces entre un cortejo de cobres.

Castillo en el aire

Ciertas tardes me salen al paso presencias insólitas. Basta rozarlas para cambiar de piel, de ojos, de instintos. Entonces me aventuro por senderos poco frecuentados. A mi derecha, grandes masas de materias impenetrables; a mi izquierda, la sucesión de fauces. Subo la montaña como se trepa esa idea fija que desde la infancia nos amedrenta y fascina y a la que, un día u otro, no tenemos más remedio que encararnos. El castillo que corona el peñasco está hecho de un solo relámpago. Esbelto y simple como un hacha, erecto y llameante, se adelanta contra el valle con la evidente intención de hendirlo. ¡Castillo de una sola pieza, proposición de lava irrefutable! ¿Se canta adentro? ¿Se ama o se degüella? El viento amontona estruendos en mi frente y el trueno establece su trono en mis tímpanos. Antes de volver a mi casa, corto la florecita que crece entre las grietas, la florecita negra quemada por el rayo.

Valle de México

El día despliega su cuerpo transparente. Atado a la piedra solar, la luz me golpea con sus grandes martillos invisibles. Sólo soy una pausa entre una vibración y otra: el punto vivo, el afilado, quieto punto fijo de intersección de dos miradas que se ignoran y se encuentran en mí. ¿Pactan? Soy el espacio puro, el campo de batalla. Veo a través de mi cuerpo mi otro cuerpo. La piedra centellea. El sol me arranca los ojos. En mis órbitas vacías dos astros alisan sus plumas rojas. Esplendor, espiral de alas y un pico feroz. Y ahora, mis ojos cantan. Asómate a su canto, arrójate a la hoguera.

waves in a thousand places at once, swan drowned in its own whiteness. You settle on the summit and nail down your lightning. And then, bending over, you kiss the frozen lips of the crater. It is time to burst in an explosion that will leave no more trace than a long scar across the sky. You cross the corridors of music and disappear into a flourish of horns.

[E.W.]

Castle in the Air

Some afternoons strange presences cross my way. A mere brush against them is enough to change skin, eyes, instincts. And then I venture on unbeaten paths. To my right, great masses of impenetrable matter; to my left, a succession of gullets. I climb the mountain the way you climb that fixed idea that since childhood has terrified and fascinated you until, one day or another, you have no choice but to face it. The castle that crowns the peak is made from a single flash of lightning. Thin and simple like an axe, erect and flaming, it advances against the valley with the apparent intention of splitting it in two. Castle of a single piece, proposition of irrefutable lava! Do they sing inside? Do they love or butcher! The wind piles clamour on my head and the thunder roots its throne in my ears. Before going home. I cut the little flower that grows between the cracks, the black flower burned by the ray.

[E.W.]

Valley of mexico

The day unfolds its transparent body. Tied to the solar stone, the light pounds me with its great invisible hammers. I am only a pause between one vibration and the next: the living point, the sharp, quiet point fixed at the intersection of two glances that ignore each other and meet within me. Do they make a pact? I am pure space, the battleground. Through my body, I see my other body. The stone sparkles. The sun rips out my eyes. Two stars smooth their red feathers in my empty sockets. Splendour, spiral of wings and a ferocious beak. And now my eyes sing. Peer into its song, throw yourself into the fire.

[E.W.]

from *Salamandra* (1958–61)

Madrugada

Rápidas manos frías
Retiran una a una
Las vendas de la sombra
Abro los ojos
           Todavía
Estoy vivo
      En el centro
De una herida todavía fresca

Aquí

Mis pasos en esta calle
Resuenan
        En otra calle
Donde
     Oigo mis pasos
Pasar en esta calle
Donde

Sólo es real la niebla

Dawn

Cold rapid hands
Draw back one by one
The bandages of dark
I open my eyes
                    Still
I am living
                At the centre
Of a wound still fresh

[C.T.]

Here

My steps along this street
Resound
            In another street
In which
            I hear my steps
Passing along this street
In which

Only the mist is real

[C.T.]

Oráculo

Los labios fríos de la noche
Dicen una palabra
Columna de pena
Piedra y no palabra
Sombra y no piedra
Pensamiento de humo
Agua real para mis labios de humo
Palabra de verdad
Razón de mis errores
Si es muerte sólo por ella vivo
Si es soledad hablo por ella
Es la memoria y no recuerdo nada
No sé lo que dice y a ella me fío
Como saberse vivo
Como olvidar que lo sabemos
Tiempo que entreabre los párpados
Y se deja mirar y nos mira

Amistad

Es la hora esperada
Sobre la mesa cae
Interminablemente
La cabellera de la lámpara
La noche vuelve inmensa la ventana
No hay nadie
La presencia sin nombre me rodea

Oracle

The cold lips of the night
Utter a word
Column of grief
No word but stone
No stone but shadow
Vaporous thought
Through my vaporous lips real water
Word of truth
Reason behind my errors
If it is death only through that do I live
If it is solitude I speak in serving it
It is memory and I remember nothing
I do not know what it says and I trust myself to it
How to know oneself living
How to forget one's knowing
Time that half-opens the eyelids
And sees us, letting itself be seen

[C.T.]

Friendship

It is the awaited hour
Over the table falls
Interminably
The lamp's spread hair
Night turns the window to immensity
There is no one here
Presence without name surrounds me

[C.T.]

Certeza

Si es real la luz blanca
De esta lámpara, real
La mano que escribe, son reales
Los ojos que miran lo escrito?

De una palabra a la otra
Lo que digo se desvanece.
Yo sé que estoy vivo
Entre dos paréntesis.

Paisaje

Peña y precipicio,
Más tiempo que piedra,
Materia sin tiempo.

Por sus cicatrices
Sin moverse cae
Perpetua agua virgen.

Reposa lo inmenso
Piedra sobre piedra,
Piedras sobre aire.

Se despliega el mundo
Tal cual es, inmóvil
Sol en el abismo.

Balanza del vértigo:
Las rocas no pesan
Más que nuestras sombras.

Certainty

If it is real the white
Light from this lamp, real
The writing hand, are they
Real, the eyes looking at what I write?

From one word to the other
What I say vanishes.
I know that I am alive
Between two parentheses

[C.T.]

Landscape

Rock and precipice,
More time than stone, this
Timeless matter.

Through its cicatrices
Falls without moving
Perpetual virgin water.

Immensity reposes here
Rock on rock,
Rocks over air.

The world's manifest
As it is: a sun
Immobile, in the abyss.

Scale of vertigo:
The crags weigh
No more than our shadows.

[C.T.]

Palpar

Mis manos
Abren las cortinas de tu ser
Te visten con otra desnudez
Descubren los cuerpos de tu cuerpo
Mis manos
Inventan otro cuerpo a tu cuerpo

Ustica

Los sucesivos soles del verano,
La sucesión del sol y sus veranos,
Todos los soles,
El solo, el sol de soles,
Hechos ya hueso terco y leonado,
Cerrazón de materia enfriada.

Puño de piedra,
Piña de lava,
Osario,
No tierra,
Isla tampoco,
Peña despeñada,
Duro durazno,
Gota de sol petrificada.

Por las noches se oye
El respirar de las cisternas,
El jadeo del agua dulce
Turbada por el mar.
La hora es alta y rayada de verde.
El cuerpo oscuro del vino

Touch

My hands
Open the curtains of your being
Clothe you in a further nudity
Uncover the bodies of your body
My hands
Invent another body for your body

[C.T.]

Ustica

The successive suns of summer,
The succession of the sun and of its summers,
All the suns,
The sole, the sol of sols
Now become
Obstinate and tawny bone,
Darkness-before-the-storm
Of matter cooled.

Fist of stone,
Pine-cone of lava,
Ossuary,
Not earth
Nor island either,
Rock off a rock-face,
Hard peach,
Sun-drop petrified.

Through the nights one hears
The breathing of cisterns,
The panting of fresh water
Troubled by the sea.
The hour is late and the light, greening.
The obscure body of the wine

En las jarras dormido
Es un sol más negro y fresco.

Aquí la rosa de las profundidades
Es un candelabro de venas rosadas
Encendido en el fondo del mar.
En tierra, el sol lo apaga,
Pálido encaje calcáreo
Como el deseo labrado por la muerte.

Rocas color de azufre,
Altas piedras adustas.
Tú estás a mi costado.
Tus pensamientos son negros y dorados.
Si alargase la mano
Cortaría un racimo de verdades intactas.
Abajo, entre peñas centelleantes,
Va y viene el mar lleno de brazos.
Vértigos. La luz se precipita.
Yo te miré a la cara,
Yo me asomé al abismo:
Mortalidad es transparencia.

Osario, paraíso:
Nuestras raíces anudadas
En el sexo, en la boca deshecha
De la Madre enterrada.
Jardín de árboles incestuosos
Sobre la tierra de los muertos.

Asleep in jars
Is a darker and cooler sun.

Here the rose of the depths
Is a candelabrum of pinkish veins
Kindled on the sea-bed.
Ashore, the sun extinguishes it,
Pale, chalky lace
As if desire were worked by death.

Cliffs the colour of sulphur,
High austere stones.
You are beside me.
Your thoughts are black and golden.
To extend a hand
Is to gather a cluster of truths intact.
Below, between sparkling rocks
Goes and comes
A sea full of arms.
Vertigoes. The light hurls itself headlong.
I looked you in the face,
I saw into the abyss:
Mortality is transparency.

Ossuary: paradise:
Our roots, knotted
In sex, in the undone mouth
Of the buried Mother.
Incestuous trees
That maintain
A garden on the dead's domain.

[c.t.]

from *Ladera este* (1962–8)

La higuera religiosa

El viento,
          Los ladrones de frutos
(Monos, pájaros,)
Entre las ramas de un gran árbol
Esparcen las semillas.
                    Verde y sonora,
La inmensa copa desbordante
Donde beben los soles
Es una entraña aérea.
                        Las semillas
Se abren,
          La planta se afinca
En el vacío,
            Hila su vértigo
Y en él se erige y se mece y propaga.
Años y años cae
                En línea recta.
Su caída
        Es el salto del agua
Congelada en el salto: tiempo petrificado.

Anda a tientas,
                Lanza largas raíces,
Varas sinuosas,
                Entrelazados
Chorros negros,
                Clava
Pilares,
        Cava húmedas galerías
Donde el eco se enciende y apaga,
Cobriza vibración
                    Resuelta en la quietud
De un sol carbonizado cada día.
Brazos, cuerdas, anillos,
                        Maraña
De mástiles y cables, encallado velero.

The Sacred Fig Tree

The wind,
      The robbers of fruit
(Monkeys, birds,)
Scatter the seeds among the branches
Of a large tree.
               Green and resonant,
The great overflowing cup
Suns drink from
Is an entrail in air.
             The seeds
Burst open,
      The plant takes hold
On emptiness,
          Spins out its vertigo
And in it grows erect and sways and breeds.
Year after year it falls
            In a straight line.
Its fall
   Is the leap of water
Frozen as it leaps: time turned to stone.

It feels its way,
          Throws out long roots
And twisting boughs,
             Black
Interlacing jets,
         It drives in
Pillars,
   Digs moist galleries
In which the echo flares and dies,
A coppery vibration
            Resolved in the stillness
Of a sun each day reduced to carbon.
Arms, cordage, rings,
         Tangle
Of masts and cables, grounded schooner.

Trepan,
  Se enroscan las raíces
Errantes.
   Es una maleza de manos.
No buscan tierra: buscan un cuerpo,
Tejen un abrazo.
    El árbol
Es un emparedado vivo.
      Su tronco
Tarda cien años en pudrirse.
       Su copa:
El cráneo mondo, las astas rotas del venado.

Bajo un manto de hojas coriáceas,
Ondulación que canta
     Del rosa al ocre al verde,
En sí misma anudada
     Dos mil años,
La higuera se arrastra, se levanta, se estrangula.

The wandering roots
                    Clamber
And coil together.
                    It is a thicket of hands.
They reach for a body, not for earth:
They are weaving an embrace.
                                        The tree
Is walled-up alive.
                    Its trunk
Takes a hundred years to rot.
                            Its top:
Bare skull, the broken antlers of a deer

Beneath a cloak of leathery leaves,
A singing wave which modulates
                            From pink to ochre to green,
Caught in its own knots
                        Two thousand years,
The fig tree crawls, grows upwards, chokes itself.

                                                    [A.T.]

AUTHOR'S NOTE

The tree in question is the pipal (*Ficus religiosus*), first cousin to the banyan (*Ficus benghalensis*). Both 'commonly start life from seed deposited by birds, squirrels, monkeys or fruit-eating bats, high upon a palm or other native tree. The roots grow downward, attached to the trunk of the supporting plant, but they are not parasitic ... The name *strangler* has become attached to fig trees which grow in this way, since their descending and encircling roots become at length largely or entirely confluent, forming a pseudo-trunk hollow at the centre through which the dead or dying host tree passes ... Roots of fig trees often enter cracks and crevices, thus causing serious injury to buildings and walls on which they are growing' (*Encyclopaedia Britannica*). The Buddhists regard the pipal as a holy tree, and it frequently appears in sculptures, paintings, poems and religious tales. Beneath its shade, Gautama perceived the truth and became the Buddha – the Enlightened One. Hence it is called the 'tree of illumination' (*boh* or *bodhi* tree). The Hindus also regard the pipal as sacred. It is associated with the Krishna cult and on its branches the god hung the clothes of the shepherdesses who were bathing in the Jamuna – a favourite theme of poets, painters and sculptors.

                                                    [A.T.]

El mausoleo de Humayun

Al debate de las avispas
La dialéctica de los monos
Górjeos de las estadísticas
Opone
          (Alta llama rosa
Hecha de piedra y aire y pájaros
Tiempo en reposo sobre el agua)

La arquitectura del silencio

En los jardines de los Lodi

En el azul unánime
Los domos de los mausoleos
– Negros, reconcentrados, pensativos –
Emitieron de pronto
                    Pájaros

The Mausoleum of Humayun

To the debate of wasps
The dialectic of monkeys
Twitterings of statistics
It opposes
        (High flame of rose
Formed out of stone and air and birds
Time in repose above the water)

Silence's architecture

                                                        [C.T.]

In the Gardens of the Lodi

Into the total blue
The domes of the mausolea
– Dark, shut round on their own thoughts –
Suddenly send forth
                Birds

                                                        [C.T.]

El otro

Se inventó una cara.
              Detrás de ella
Vivió, murió y resucitó
Muchas veces.
              Su cara
Hoy tiene las arrugas de esa cara.
Sus arrugas no tienen cara.

The Other

He invented a face for himself.
                              Behind it,
He lived, died, and resurrected,
Many times.
              His face today
Has the wrinkles of that face.
His wrinkles have no face.

[E.W.]

Golden Lotuses (2)

Delgada y sinuosa
Como la cuerda mágica.
Rubia y rauda:
                    Dardo y milano.
Pero también inexorable rompehielos.
Senos de niña, ojos de esmalte.
Bailó en todas las terrazas y sótanos,
Contempló un atardecer en San José, Costa Rica,
Durmió en las rodillas de los Himalayas,
Fatigó los bares y las sabanas de África.
A los veinte dejó a su marido
Por una alemana;
A los veintiuno dejó a la alemana
Por un afgano;
A los cuarenta y cinco
Vive en Proserpina Court, int. 2, Bombay.
Cada mes, en los días rituales,
Llueven sapos y culebras en la casa,
Los criados maldicen a la demonia
Y su amante *parsi* apaga el fuego.
Tempestad en seco.
                    El buitre blanco
Picotea su sombra.

Golden Lotuses (2)

Lithe and sinuous
Like the magical string.
Swift and blond:
        Lance and kite.
But also inexorable ice-breaker.
Breasts of a child, eyes of enamel.
She danced through all the terraces and cellars,
Observed a sunset in San José, Costa Rica,
Slept on the knees of the Himalayas,
Left the saloons and savannahs of Africa wilting.
At twenty she left her husband
For a Fräulein;
At twenty-one she left the Fräulein
For an Afghan;
At forty-five
She lives in Proserpina Court, int. 2, Bombay.
Each month, on holy-days,
The place jumps with natterjacks and snakes,
The servants curse her for a fiend
And her Parsee lover quells the fire.
Storm without rain.
        The white vulture
Picks at its shadow.

                         [M.E.]

Utacamud

1

En las montañas Nilgiri
Busqué a los Toda.
Sus templos son establos cónicos.
Flacos, barbudos y herméticos,
Al ordeñar sus búfalos sagrados
Salmodian himnos incoherentes.
Desde Sumaria guardan un secreto
Sin saber que lo guardan
Y entre los labios resecos de los viejos
El nombre de Ishtar, diosa cruel,
Brilla como la luna sobre un pozo vacío.

2

En la veranda del Cecil Hotel
Miss Penélope (pelo canario,
Medias de lana, báculo) repite
Desde hace treinta años: *Oh India,*
Country of missed opportunities . . .
Arriba,
Entre los fuegos de artificio
De la jacaranda,
                    Graznan los cuervos,
Alegremente.

3

Altas yerbas y árboles bajos.
Territorio indeciso. En los claros
Las termitas aladas construyen
Diminutos castillos ciclópeos.
Homenajes de arena
A Micenas y Macchu-Picchu.

Utacamud

On the Nilgiri Hills
I looked for the Toda.
Their temples are conical stables.
Bony, bearded and inscrutable,
They milk their sacred buffaloes
While droning incoherent hymns.
They preserve a secret from Sumer
Not knowing they preserve it
And between the dried-up lips of the ancients
The name of Ishtar, the cruel goddess,
Gleams like a shard of moonlight on an empty well.

2

On the verandah of the Cecil Hotel
Miss Penelope (canary hair,
Walking-stick, woollen hose) has been
Repeating these thirty years: *Oh India,*
Country of missed opportunities ...
Overhead,
Amid the jacaranda's
Firework display
                    The gay
Caws of the crows.

3

Tall grasses and short trees.
Uncertain ground. In the clearings
The flying termites build
Minute cyclopean castles.
Homages in sand
To Mycenae and Macchu-Picchu.

4

Más hojoso y brillante
El *nim* es como el fresno:
Es un árbol cantante.

5

Visión en el desfiladero:
El árbol de camelias rosa
Doblado sobre el precipicio.
Fulgor entre verdores taciturnos
Plantado en un abismo.
Una presencia impenetrable,
Indiferente al vértigo – y al lenguaje.

6

Crece en la noche el cielo,
Eucalipto encendido.
Estrellas generosas:
No me aplastan, me llaman.

4

More shining and leafy
The *nim* is like the ash:
It is a singing tree.

5

A vision along the pass:
The rose camellia tree
Tilted over the chasm.
Effulgence amid taciturn greens
Planted on falling space.
Impenetrable presence,
Careless of vertigo – and of language.

6

The sky grows in the night,
A eucalyptus kindled.
Magnanimous constellations:
Not crushing me – calling.

[M.E.]

Cerca del Cabo Comorín

En un *land-rover* averiado
En mitad del campo llovido.
Árboles con el agua al cuello
Bajo un cielo recién nacido
Y blancos pájaros flemáticos,
Airones y garzotas, impolutos
Entre tantos verdes dramáticos.
En la ciénaga sumergidos
Estultos búfalos lustrosos comen,
Casi enteramente dormidos,
Lirios acuáticos.
                    Una pandilla
De monos mendicantes. Increíble
Mente trepada, una cabra amarilla
Sobre una piedra puntiaguda. Un cuervo
Sobre la cabra. Y la invisible,
Aunque constante, pánica presencia:
No araña o cobra, lo Innominable,
La universal indiferencia
Donde la forma vil y la adorable
Prosperan y se anulan: vacíos hervideros.
Doble latido en la fijeza del espacio:
El sol junto a la luna. Anochece.
El martín pescador es un topacio
Instantáneo. El carbón prevalece.
Se disuelve el paisaje ahogado.
¿Soy alma en pena o cuerpo errante?
Se disuelve también el *land-rover* parado.

Near Cape Comorin

In a Land Rover, broken down
Midway through flooded fields.
Trees up to their necks in water
Beneath a newborn sky
And white, phlegmatic birds,
Egrets and heron, immaculate
Among all these dramatic greens.
Submerged in mire,
Sleek, mindless buffaloes,
Practically asleep,
Are eating water lilies.
                    A troupe
Of begging monkeys. Poised
Incredibly, a yellow goat
Upon a pointed rock. Upon the goat,
A raven. And the invisible,
Yet constant, panic presence:
Not spider or cobra, the Unnameable,
The universal apathy
In which the base form and the godlike
Thrive and negate each other: vacant swarms.
Twin pulse within the fixity of space:
Conjunction of sun and moon. It is getting dark.
The kingfisher is a flash
Of topaz. Carbon dominates.
The drowned landscape dissolves.
Am I a lost soul or a wandering body?
The stalled Land Rover likewise dissolves.

[A.T.]

Felicidad en Herat

A Carlos Pellicer

Vine aquí
Como escribo estas líneas,
Sin idea fija:
Una mezquita azul y verde,
Seis minaretes truncos,
Dos o tres tumbas,
Memorias de un poeta santo,
Los nombres de Timur y su linaje.

Encontré al viento de los cien días.
Todas las noches las cubrió de arena,
Acosó mi frente, me quemó los párpados.
La madrugada:
                        Dispersión de pájaros
Y ese rumor de agua entre piedras
Que son los pasos campesinos.
(Pero el agua sabía a polvo.)
Murmullos en el llano,
Apariciones
                Desapariciones,
Ocres torbellinos
Insustanciales como mis pensamientos.
Vueltas y vueltas
En un cuarto de hotel o en las colinas:
La tierra un cementerio de camellos
Y en mis cavilaciones siempre
Los mismos rostros que se desmoronan.
El viento, el señor de las ruinas,
Es mi único maestro?
Erosiones:
El menos crece más y más.

En la tumba del santo,
Hondo en el árbol seco,
Clavé un clavo,

Happiness in Herat

To Carlos Pellicer

I came here
As I write these lines,
At random:
A blue-and-green mosque,
Six truncated minarets,
Two or three tombs,
Memories of a poet-saint,
The names of Timur and his lineage.

I met the wind of the hundred days.
It spread sand over all the nights.
It scourged my brow, scorched my lids.
Daybreak:
            Dispersion of birds
And that sound of water among stones
Which is the peasant's footsteps.
(But the water tasted of dust.)
Murmurs in the plain,
Appearances
            Disappearances,
Ochre whirlwinds
Insubstantial as my thoughts.
Wheeling and wheeling
In the hotel room, on the hills:
This land a camels' graveyard
And in my brooding
Always the same crumbling faces:
Is the wind, the lord of ruins,
My only master?
Erosions:
Minus grows more and more.

At the saint's tomb
I nailed a nail
Deep into the lifeless tree,

No,
Como los otros, contra el mal de ojo:
Contra mi mismo.
                (Algo dije:
Palabras que se lleva el viento.)

Una tarde pactaron las alturas.
Sin cambiar de lugar
                    Caminaron los chopos.
Sol en los azulejos
                    Súbitas primaveras.
En el Jardín de las Señoras
Subí a la cúpula turquesa.
Minaretes tatuados de signos:
La escritura cúfica, más allá de la letra,
Se volvió transparente.
No tuve la visión sin imágenes,
No ví girar las formas hasta desvanecerse
En claridad inmóvil,
El ser ya sin sustancia del sufí.
No bebí plenitud en el vacío
Ni ví las treinta y dos señales
Del Bodisatva cuerpo de diamante.
Ví un cielo azul y todos los azules,
Del blanco al verde
Todo el abanico de los álamos
Y sobre el pino, más aire que pájaro,
El mirlo blanquinegro.
Vi al mundo reposar en si mismo.
Vi las apariencias.
Y llamé a esa media hora:
Perfección de lo Finito.

                    Not,
Like the others, against the evil eye:
Against myself.
(I said something –
Words the wind took away.)

One afternoon the heights convened.
The poplars walked around
                              While standing still.
Sun on the glazed tiles
                    Sudden springtimes.
In the Ladies' Garden
I climbed to the turquoise cupola.
Minarets tattooed with characters:
That Cufic script became clear
Beyond its meaning.
I did not have the vision without images,
I did not see forms whirl till they disappeared
In immobile clarity,
In the Sufi's being-without-substance.
I did not drink plenitude in vacuity
Nor see the two and thirty signs
Of the Bodhisattva's diamond-body.
I saw a blue sky and all the shades of blue,
And the white to green
Of the spread fan of the poplars,
And, on the tip of the pine tree,
The black-and-white ouzel,
Less bird than air.
I saw the world resting upon itself.
I saw the appearances.
And I named that half-hour:
Perfection of the Finite.

                                        [L.K.]

Efectos del bautismo

El joven Hassan,
Por casarse con una cristiana,
Se bautizó.
        El cura,
Como a un vikingo,
Lo llamó Erik.
          Ahora
Tiene dos nombres
Y una sola mujer.

Aparición

Si el hombre es polvo
Esos que andan por el llano
Son hombres

Results of Baptism

Young Hassan
In order to marry a Christian
Got baptized.
           As though he were a Viking,
The priest
Named him Eric.
              Now
He has two names
And only one wife.

                                        [C.T.]

Apparition

If man is dust
Those who go through the plain
Are men

                                        [C.T.]

Pueblo

Las piedras son tiempo
                        El viento
Siglos de viento
                Los árboles son tiempo
Las gentes son piedra
                        El viento
Vuelve sobre si mismo y se entierra
En el día de piedra

No hay agua pero brillan los ojos

Village

The stones are time
                    The wind
Centuries of wind
                    The trees are time
The people are stone
                    The wind
Turns upon itself and sinks
Into the stone day

There is no water here for all the lustre of its eyes

[C.T.]

Vrindaban

Rodeado de noche
Follaje inmenso de rumores
Grandes cortinas impalpables
Hálitos
       Escribo me detengo
Escribo
       (Todo está y no está
Todo calladamente se desmorona
Sobre la página)
           Hace unos instantes
Corría en un coche
Entre las casas apagadas
          Corría
Entre mis pensamientos encendidos
Arriba las estrellas
         Jardines serenísimos
Yo era un árbol y hablaba
Estaba cubierto de hojas y ojos
Yo era el murmullo que avanza
El enjambre de imágenes
(Ahora trazo unos cuantos signos
Crispados
       Negro sobre blanco
Diminuto jardín de letras
A la luz de una lámpara plantado)
Corría el coche
Por los barrios dormidos yo corría
Tras de mis pensamientos
             Míos y de los otros
Reminiscencias supervivencias figuraciones
Nombres
     Los restos de las chispas
     Y las risas de la velada
     La danza de las horas
     La marcha de las constelaciones

Vrindaban

Surrounded by night
Immense forest of breathing
Vast impalpable curtains
Murmurs
        I write
I stop
     I write
         (All is and is not
And it all falls apart on the page
In silence)
        A moment ago
A car raced down the street
Among the extinguished houses
             I raced
Among my lighted thoughts
Above me the stars
          Such quiet gardens
I was a tree and spoke
Was covered with leaves and eyes
Was the rumour pushing forward
A swarm of images
(I set down now a few
Twisted strokes
        Black on white
Diminutive garden of letters
Planted in the lamp's light)
The car raced on
Through the sleeping suburb
          I raced
To follow my thoughts
        Mine and others
Reminiscences Left-overs Imaginings
Names
    The remains of sparks
    The laughter of the late parties
    The dance of the hours
    The march of the constellations

Y otros lugares comunes
Yo creo en los hombres
                    O en los astros?
Yo creo
        (Aquí intervienen los puntos
Suspensivos)
                Yo veo

Pórtico de columnas carcomidas
Estatuas esculpidas por la peste
La doble fila de mendigos
                        Y el hedor
Rey en su trono
                Rodeado
Como si fuesen concubinas
Por un vaivén de aromas
Puros casi corpóreos ondulantes
Del sándalo al jazmín y sus fantasmas
Putrefacción
                Fiebre de formas
                        Fiebre del tiempo
En sus combinaciones extasiado
Cola de pavo real el universo entero
Miríadas de ojos
                En otros ojos reflejados
Modulaciones reverberaciones de un ojo único
Un solitario sol
                Oculto
Tras su manto de transparencias
Su marea de maravillas
Todo llameaba
                Piedras mujeres agua
Todo se esculpía
                Del color a la forma
De la forma al incendio
                    Todo se desvanecía
Música de metales y maderas
En la celda del dios
                Matriz del templo
Música de soles enlazados

And other commonplaces
Do I believe in man
    Or in the stars?
I believe
  (With here a series
Of dots)
   I see

A portico of weather-eaten pillars
Statues carved by the plague
It is a double line of beggars
      The stench
A king on his throne
     Surrounded
By a coming and going of aromas
As if they were concubines
Pure almost corporeal undulating
From the sandalwood to the jasmine
And its phantoms
    Fever of forms
      Fever of time
Ecstatic in its combinations
The whole universe a peacock's tail
Myriads of eyes
    Other eyes reflecting
Modulations
    Reverberations of a single eye
A solitary sun
   Hidden
Behind its cloth of transparencies
Its tide of marvels
Everything was flaming
     Stones women water
Everything sculptured
     From colour to form
From form to fire
    Everything was vanishing
Music of wood and metal
In the cell of the god
    Womb of the temple
Music like spliced suns

Música
Como el agua y el viento en sus abrazos
Y sobre las materias que gemían
Confundidas
                    La voz humana
Luna en celo por el mediodía
Queja del alma que se desencarna
(Escribo sin conocer el desenlace
De lo que escribo
                        Busco entre líneas
Mi imagen es la lámpara
                            Encendida
En mitad de la noche)
                        Saltimbanqui
Mono de lo Absoluto
                    Garabato
En cuclillas
            Cubierto de cenizas pálidas
Un sadú me miraba y se reía
Desde su orilla me miraba
                        Lejos lejos
Como los animales y los santos me miraba
Desnudo desgreñado embadurnado
Un rayo fijo los ojos minerales
Yo quise hablarle
Me respondió con borborigmos
                            Ido ido
Adónde
        A qué región del ser
A qué existencia a la intemperie de qué mundos
En qué tiempo?
                (Escribo
Cada letra es un germen
                        La memoria
Insiste en su marea
Y repite su mismo mediodía)
Ido ido
        Santo pícaro santo
Arrobos del hambre o de la droga
Tal vez vio a Krishna

Music
Like the wind and water embracing
And over the confused moans
Of matter
                The human voice
A moon in heat at midday
Complaint of the disembodied soul
(I write without knowing the outccme
Of what I write
                        I look between the lines
My image is the lamp
                Lit
In the middle of the night)
                        Mountebank
Ape of the absolute
                Cowering
Pothook
        Covered with pale ashes
A sadhu looked at me and laughed
Watching me from the other shore
                                · Far off, far off
Watching me like the animals like the saints
Naked uncombed smeared
A fixed ray a mineral glitter his cyes
I wanted to speak to him
He answered with a rumble of bowels
                                Gone   gone
Where?
        To what region of being
To what existence
                In the open air of what worlds
In what time?
                (I write
Each letter is a germ
                        The memory
Imposes its tide
And repeats its own midday)
Gone gone
                Saint   scoundrel   saint
In beatitudes of hunger or drugs
Perhaps he saw Krishna

Arbol azul y centelleante
Nocturno surtidor brotando en la sequía
Tal vez en una piedra hendida
Palpó la forma femenina
                        Y su desgarradura
El vértigo sin forma
                    Por esto o aquello
Vive en el muelle donde queman a los muertos

Las calles solas
Las casas y sus sombras
Todo era igual y todo era distinto
El coche corría
                    Yo estaba quieto
Entre mis pensamientos desbocados
(Ido ido
Santo payaso santo mendigo rey maldito
Es lo mismo
                    Siempre lo mismo
                                En lo mismo
Es ser siempre en sí mismo
                                Encerrado
En lo mismo
                    En sí mismo cerrado
Idolo podrido)
                Ido ido
Desde su orilla me miraba
                            Me mira
Desde su interminable mediodía
Yo estoy en la hora inestable
El coche corre entre las casas
Yo escribo a la luz de una lámpara
Los absolutos las eternidades
Y sus aledaños
                    No son mi tema
Tengo hambre de vida y también de morir
Sé lo que creo y lo escribo
Advenimientos del instante
                            El acto
El movimiento en que se esculpe
Y se deshace el ser entero

                    Sparkling blue tree
Dark fountain splashing amid the drought
Perhaps in a cleft stone
He grasped the form of woman
                              Its rent
The formless dizziness
                    For this or that
He lives on the ghat where they burn the dead

The lonely streets
The houses and their shadows
All was the same and all different
The car raced on
                    I was quiet
Among my runaway thoughts
(Gone   gone
Saint   clown   saint   beggar   king   damned
It is the same
                Always the same
                              Within the same
It is to be always within oneself
Closed up in the same
                    Closed up on oneself
Rotted idol)
            Gone   gone
He watched me from the other shore
                              He watches me

From his interminable noon
I am in the wandering hour
The car races on among the houses
I write by the light of a lamp
The absolutes the eternities
Their outlying districts
                    Are not my theme
I am hungry for life and for death also
I know what I know and I write it
The embodiment of time
                    The act
The movement in which the whole being
Is sculptured and destroyed

Conciencia y manos para asir el tiempo
Soy una historia
                Una memoria que se inventa
Nunca estoy solo
Hablo siempre contigo Hablas siempre conmigo
A oscuras voy y planto signos

Consciousness and hands to grasp the hour
I am a history
                    A memory inventing itself
I am never alone
I speak with you always
                          You speak with me always
I move in the dark
                    I plant signs

[L.K.]

Himachal Pradesh (3)

5 pequeñas abominaciones
vistas, oídas, cometidas:

El festín de los buitres.
Comieron tanto que no pueden volar.
No muy lejos, sobre una peña,
un águila tullida
espera su resto de carroña.

El *barrister* de Nagpur pesca al extranjero
en la veranda del *dak bungalow* y le ofrece,
en un inglés enmelado, un trago, un cesto
de ciruelas de su huerta, un mapa, un
almuerzo de *curry*, noticias verídicas del país,
el balcón de su casa con una vista
única . . . Su mujer lo observa, oblicua,
mascullando injurias en hindustani.

Ya por tomar el fresco o sorprender
ese momento de armisticio
en que la media luna es verdadera
mente blanca y el sol es todavía
el sol, se asoma al aire la pareja
de viejitos. Se animan, resucitan
una pasión feroz de insectos.
Sonaja de semillas secas:
la hora de las recriminaciones.

En el patio del club seis eucaliptos
se ahogan en una casi luz casi miel,
tres ingleses supervivientes del *British Raj*
comentan con un *sikh* el *match* de *cricket* en Sidney,
unas matronas indias juegan *bridge*, un paria
lava el piso en cuclillas y se eclipsa,
un astro negro se abre en mi frente
como una granada (EN PARÍS PRENDEN FUEGO
A LA BOLSA, TEMPLO DEL CAPITALISMO),
los pinos ensombrecen la colina.

Himachal Pradesh (3)

5 minor abominations
seen, heard, committed:

The banquet of the vultures.
They fed so well they're too heavy to fly.
From his boulder,
not far off a crippled eagle
watches for his leavings of carrion.

The legal johnnie from Nagpur hooks the foreigner
on the verandah of the dak bungalow and offers him,
in a honeyed English, a tiff, a basket
of plums from his garden, a map, a
bite of curry, reliable news of the region,
the balcony of his house with a quite
unique view . . . His wife observes him, obliquely,
muttering insults in Hindustani.

Now, to take the air or to surprise
that moment of détente
when the half moon is real
ly white and the sun is still
the sun, the pair of sweet old men appears.
They get excited, resurrect
a fierce insect passion.
Rattle of dry seeds:
an hour for recriminations.

In the lobby at the club six eucalypti
gasp in the dubious, syrupy light,
three Englishmen, survivors from the Raj,
dissect the Sydney Test with a Sikh,
Indian dowagers play bridge, a pariah,
squatting, washes the floor and disappears,
a black star explodes in my brain,
a grenade (IN PARIS THEY'RE BURNING
THE BOURSE, THE TEMPLE OF CAPITALISM),
the pines shadow the hill.

Polvo y gritos de pájaros
sobre la tarde quemada.
Yo escribo estas líneas infames.

Dust and bird-cries
on the burnt evening.
I write these infamous lines.

Tumba del poeta

El libro
   El vaso
El verde oscuramente tallo
      El disco
La bella durmiente en su lecho de música
Las cosas anegadas en sus nombres
Decirlas con los ojos
      En un allá no se donde
Clavarlas
   Lámpara lápiz retrato
Esto que veo
    Clavarlo
Como un templo vivo
      Plantarlo
Como un árbol
    Un dios
Coronarlo
   Con un nombre
      Inmortal
Irrisoria corona de espinas
      Lenguaje!
El tallo y su flor inminente
      Sol-sexo-sol
La flor sin sombra
    En un allá sin donde
Se abre
   Como el horizonte
      Se abre
La extensión inmaculada
Transparencia que sostiene a las cosas
Caídas
  Por la mirada
Levantadas
   En un reflejo
      Suspendidas
Lunas multiplicadas

Tomb of the Poet

The book
      The glass
The green obscurely a stalk
             The record
Sleeping beauty in her bed of music
Things drowned in their names
To say them with the eyes
           In a beyond I cannot tell where
Nail them down
        Lamp pencil portrait
This that I see
      To nail it down
Like a living temple
        Plant it
Like a tree
    A god
Crown it
    With a name
        Immortal
Derisible crown of thorns
        Speech!
The stalk and its imminent flower
           Sun-sex-sun
The flower without shadow
         In a beyond without where
Opens
    Like the horizon
        Opens
Immaculate extension
Transparency which sustains things
Fallen
    Raised up
By the glance
      Held
        In a reflection
Moons multiplied

                    En la estepa
Haz de mundos
                Instantes
Racimos encendidos
Selvas andantes de astros
Sílabas errantes
Milenios de arena cayendo sin término
                                Marca
Todos los tiempos del tiempo
                            SER
Una fracción de segundo
                        Lámpara lápiz retrato
En un aquí no se donde
                        Un nombre
Comienza
        Asirlo plantarlo decirlo
Como un bosque pensante
                        Encarnarlo
Un linaje comienza
                    En un nombre
Un adán
        Como un templo vivo
Nombre sin sombra
                    Clavado
Como un dios
            En este aquí sin donde
Lenguaje!
        Acabo en su comienzo
En esto que digo
                Acabo
SER
    Sombra de un nombre instántaneo

NUNCA SABRE MI DESENLACE

                    Across the steppe
Bundle of worlds
                    Instants
Glowing bunches
Moving forests of stars
Wandering syllables
Millennia of sand endlessly falling away
                                    Tide
All the time of time
                          TO BE
A second's fraction
                    Lamp pencil portrait
In a here I cannot tell where
                          A name
Begins
        Seize on it, plant, say it
Like a wood that thinks
                    Flesh it
A lineage begins
                In a name
An adam
        Like a living temple
Name without shadow
                    Nailed
Like a god
            In this here-without-where
Speech!
        I cease in its beginning
In this that I say
                I cease
TO BE
        Shadow of an instantaneous name

I SHALL NEVER KNOW MY BOND'S UNDOING

                                              [C.T.]

Madrugada al raso

Los labios y las manos del viento
El corazón del agua
                            Un eucalipto
El campamento de las nubes
La vida que nace cada día
La muerte que nace cada vida

Froto mis párpados:
El cielo anda en la tierra

La exclamación

Quieto
            No en la rama
En el aire
                No en el aire
En el instante
                El colibrí

Próximo lejano

Anoche un fresno
A punto de decirme
Algo – callóse

Daybreak

Hands and lips of the wind
Heart of the water
                 A eucalyptus
Campground of the clouds
The life that is born every day
The death that is born every life

I rub my eyes:
The sky walks the land

                                         [E.W.]

Exclamation

Still
    Not on the branch
In the air
         Not in the air
In the instant
           The hummingbird

                                           [C.T.]

Distant Neighbour

Last night an ash-tree
Was about to say –
But it didn't

                                         [E.W.]

Lo idéntico

(*Anton Webern, 1883–1945*)

Espacios
      Espacio
Sin centro ni arriba ni abajo
Se devora y se engendra y no cesa
Espacio remolino
               Y caída hacia arriba
Espacios
      Claridades cortadas a pico
Suspendidas
        Al flanco de la noche
Jardines negros de cristal de roca
En una vara de humo florecidos
Jardines blancos que estallan en el aire
Espacios
     Un solo espacio que se abre
Corola
    Y se disuelve
Espacio en el espacio
             Todo es ninguna parte
Lugar de las nupcias impalpables

Escritura

Yo dibujo estas letras
Como el día dibuja sus imágenes
Y sopla sobre ellas y no vuelve

One and the Same

(Anton Webern, 1883–1945)

Spaces
    Space
Without centre no above or below
Devours and engenders itself and does not cease
Whirlpool space
            And it falls into height
Spaces
    Clarities
Cut into jewel-points
            Hanging
From night's sheerness
Black gardens of rock crystal
Flowering along a bough of smoke
White gardens that explode in air
Spaces
    A sole space that unfolds
Flower-face
       And dissolves
Space into space
All is nowhere
Place of impalpable nuptials

           [C.T.]

Writing

I draw these letters
As the day draws its images
And blows over them
       And does not return

           [E.W.]

Concorde

A Carlos Fuentes

Arriba el agua
Abajo el bosque
El viento por los caminos

Quietud del pozo
El cubo es negro El agua firme

El agua baja hasta los árboles
El cielo sube hasta los labios

Juventud

El salto de la ola
                    Más blanca
Cada hora
            Más verde
Cada día
            Más joven
La muerte

Concord

To Carlos Fuentes

      Water above
      Grove below
Wind on the roads

      Quiet well
Bucket's black Still water

Water descending to the trees
Sky rising to the lips

                           [E.W.]

Youth

The leap of the wave
               Whiter
Each hour
         Greener
Each day
      Younger
Death

                           [C.T.]

Viento entero

El presente es perpetuo
Los montes son de hueso y son de nieve
Están aquí desde el principio
El viento acaba de nacer
                    Sin edad
Como la luz y como el polvo
                         Molino de sonidos
El bazar tornasolea
                    Timbres motores radios
El trote pétreo de los asnos opacos
Cantos y quejas enredados
Entre las barbas de los comerciantes
Alto fulgor a martillazos esculpido
En los claros de silencio
                    Estallan
Los gritos de los niños
                    Príncipes en harapos
A la orilla del río atormentado
Rezan orinan meditan
                    El presente es perpetuo
Se abren las compuertas del año
                         El día salta
        Agata
        El pájaro caído
Entre la calle Montalambert y la de Bac
Es una muchacha
                    Detenida
Sobre un precipicio de miradas
Si el agua es fuego
                    Llama
En el centro de la hora redonda
                         Encandilada
        Potranca alazana
Un haz de chispas
                    Una muchacha real
Entre las casas y las gentes espectrales
Presencia chorro de evidencias
Yo ví a través de mis actos irreales

Wind from all Compass Points

The present is motionless
The mountains are of bone and of snow
They have been here since the beginning
The wind has just been born
                              Ageless
As the light and the dust
                         A windmill of sounds
The bazaar spins its colours
                              Bells   motors   radios
The stony trot of dark donkeys
Songs and complaints entangled
Among the beards of the merchants
The tall light chiselled with hammer-strokes
In the clearings of silence
                         Boys' cries
      Explode
Princes in tattered clothes
On the banks of the tortured river
Pray   pee   meditate
                              The present is motionless
The floodgates of the year open
                              Day flashes out
            Agate
      The fallen bird
Between rue Montalambert and rue de Bac
Is a girl
         Held back
At the edge of a precipice of looks
If water is fire
                Flame
                Dazzled
In the centre of the spherical hour
                A sorrel filly
A marching battalion of sparks
                              A real girl
Among wraithlike houses and people
Presence a fountain of reality
I looked out through my own unrealities

La tomé de la mano
     Juntos atravesamos
Los cuatro espacios los tres tiempos
Pueblos errantes de reflejos
Y volvimos al día del comienzo
El presente es perpetuo
      21 de junio
Hoy comienza el verano
       Dos o tres pájaros
Inventan un jardín
      Tú lees y comes un durazno
Sobre la colcha roja
     Desnuda
Como el vino en el cántaro de vidrio
      Un gran vuelo de cuervos
En Santo Domingo mueren nuestros hermanos
'Si hubiera parque no estarían ustedes aquí'
     Nosotros nos roemos los codos
En los jardines de su alcázar de estío
Tipú Sultán plantó el árbol de los jacobinos
Luego distribuyó pedazos de vidrio
Entre los oficiales ingleses prisioneros
Y ordenó que se cortasen el prepucio
Y se lo comiesen
    El presente es perpetuo
El sol se ha dormido entre tus pechos
La colcha roja es negra y palpita
Ni astro ni alhaja
    Fruta
Tú te llamas dátil
    Datia
Castillo de sal si puedes
     Mancha escarlata
Sobre la piedra empedernida
Galerías terrazas escaleras
Desmanteladas salas nupciales
Del escorpión

I took her hand
                    Together we crossed
The four quadrants the three times
Floating tribes of reflections
And we returned to the day of beginning
The present is motionless
                                June 21st
Today is the beginning of summer
                                    Two or three birds
Invent a garden
                    You read and eat a peach
On the red couch
                    Naked
Like the wine in the glass pitcher
                                A great flock of crows
Our brothers are dying in Santo Domingo
'If we had the munitions
                    You people would not be here'
                We chew our nails down to the elbow
In the gardens of his summer fortress
Tipoo Sultan planted the Jacobin tree
Then distributed glass shards among
The imprisoned English officers
And ordered them to cut their foreskins
And eat them
                    The present is motionless
The sun has fallen asleep between your breasts
The red covering is black and heaves
Not planet and not jewel
                            Fruit
You are named
                Date
                Datia
Castle of Leave-If-You-Can
                            Scarlet stain
Upon the obdurate stone
Corridors
            Terraces
                Stairways
Dismantled nuptial chambers
Of the scorpion

Ecos repeticiones
Relojería erótica
Deshora
Tú recorres
Los patios taciturnos bajo la tarde impía
Manto de agujas en tus hombros indemnes
Si el fuego es agua
Eres una gota diáfana
La muchacha real
Transparencia del mundo
El presente es perpetuo
Los montes
Soles destazados
Petrificada tempestad ocre
El viento rasga
Ver duele
El cielo es otro abismo más alto
Garganta de Salang
La nube negra sobre la roca negra
El puño de la sangre golpea
Puertas de piedra
Sólo el agua es humana
En estas soledades despeñadas
Sólo tus ojos de agua humana
Abajo
En el espacio hendido
El deseo te cubre con sus dos alas negras
Tus ojos se abren y se cierran
Animales fosforescentes
Abajo
El desfiladero caliente
La ola que se dilata y se rompe
Tus piernas abiertas
El salto blanco
La espuma de nuestros cuerpos abandonados
El presente es perpetuo
El morabito regaba la tumba del santo
Sus barbas eran más blancas que las nubes
Frente al moral
Al flanco del torrente
Repetiste mi nombre

Echoes repetitions
The intricate and erotic works of a watch
                                    Beyond time
                                        You cross
Taciturn patios under the pitiless afternoon
A cloak of needles on your untouched shoulders
If fire is water
                        You are a diaphanous drop
The real girl
                    Transparency of the world
The present is motionless
                            The mountains
                    Quartered suns
Petrified storm earth-yellow
                        The wind whips
                                It hurts to see
The sky is another deeper abyss
                        Gorge of the Salang Pass
Black cloud over black rock
Fist of blood strikes
                        Gates of stone
Only the water is human
In these precipitous solitudes
Only your eyes of human water
                            Down there
In the cleft
Desire covers you with its two black wings
Your eyes flash open and close
                            Phosphorescent animals
Down there
                The hot canyon
The wave that stretches and breaks
                            Your legs apart
The plunging whiteness
The foam of our bodies abandoned
                            The present is motionless
The hermit watered the saint's tomb
His beard was whiter than the clouds
Facing the mulberry
                    On the flank of the rushing stream
You repeat my name

Dispersión de sílabas
Un adolescente de ojos verdes te regaló
Una granada
                    Al otro lado del Amu-Darya
Humeaban las casitas rusas
El son de la flauta usbek
Era otro río invisible y más puro
En la barcaza el batelero estrangulaba pollos
El país es una mano abierta
                            Sus líneas
        Signos de un alfabeto roto
Osamentas de vacas en el llano
Bactriana
            Estatua pulverizada
Yo recogí del polvo unos cuantos nombres
Por esas sílabas caídas
Granos de una granada cenicienta
Juro ser tierra y viento
                    Remolino
Sobre tus huesos
                    El presente es perpetuo
La noche entra con todos sus árboles
Noche de insectos eléctricos y fieras de seda
Noche de yerbas que andan sobre los muertos
Conjunción de aguas que vienen de lejos
Murmullos
            Los universos se desgranan
Un mundo cae
                    Se enciende una semilla
Cada palabra palpita
                        Oigo tu latir en la sombra
Enigma en forma de reloj de arena
                            Mujer dormida
Espacio espacios animados
Anima mundi
                Materia maternal
Perpetua desterrada de sí misma
Y caída perpetua en su entraña vacía
                            Anima mundi
Madre de las razas errantes

Dispersion of syllables

A young man with green eyes presented you
With a pomegranate
                    On the other bank of the Amu-Darya
Smoke rose from Russian cottages
The sound of an Usbek flute
Was another river invisible clearer
The boatman
                    On the barge was strangling chickens
The countryside is an open hand
                                        Its lines
                    Marks of a broken alphabet
Cow skeletons on the prairie
Bactria
        A shattered statue
I scraped a few names out of the dust
By these fallen syllables
Seeds of a charred pomegranate
I swear to be earth and wind
                    Whirling
Over your bones
                    The present is motionless
Night comes down with its trees
Night of electric insects and silken beasts
Night of grasses which cover the dead
Meeting of waters which come from far off
Rustlings
        Universes are strewn about
A world falls
            A seed flares up
Each word beats
                    I hear you throb in the shadow
A riddle shaped like an hour-glass
                        Woman asleep
Space   living spaces
Anima mundi
            Maternal substance
Always torn from itself
Always falling into your empty womb
                        Anima mundi
Mother of the nomadic tribes

                    De soles y de hombres
Emigran los espacios
                    El presente es perpetuo
En el pico del mundo se acarician
Shiva y Parvati
                    Cada caricia dura un siglo
Para el dios y para el hombre
                              Un mismo tiempo
Un mismo despeñarse
                    Lahor
                              Río rojo barcas negras
Entre dos tamarindos una niña descalza
Y su mirar sin tiempo
                    Un latido idéntico
Muerte y nacimiento
Entre el cielo y la tierra suspendidos
Unos cuantos álamos
Vibrar de luz más que vaivén de hojas
                              Suben o bajan?
El presente es perpetuo
                    Llueve sobre mi infancia
Llueve sobre el jardín de la fiebre
Flores de sílex árboles de humo
En una hoja de higuera tú navegas
Por mi frente
            La lluvia no te moja
Eres la llama de agua
                    La gota diáfana de fuego
Derramada sobre mis párpados
Yo veo a través de mis actos irreales
El mismo día que comienza
                    Gira el espacio
Arranca sus raíces el mundo
No pesan más que el alba nuestros cuerpos
                              Tendidos

<pre>
                    Of suns and men
The spaces turn
                The present is motionless
At the top of the world
Shiva and Parvati caress
                        Each caress lasts a century
For the god and for the man
                        An identical time
An equivalent hurling headling
                    Lahore
                        Red river black boats
A barefoot girl
            Between two tamarinds
And her timeless gaze
                An identical throbbing
Death and birth
A group of poplars
Suspended between sky and earth
They are a quiver of light more than a trembling of leaves
                Do they rise
                        Or fall?
The present is motionless
                It rains on my childhood
It rains on the feverish garden
Flint flowers   trees of smoke
In a fig-leaf you sail
                On my brow
The rain does not wet you
You are flame of water
                    The diaphanous drop of fire
Spilling upon my eyelids
I look out through my own unrealities
The same day is beginning
                        Space wheels
The world wrenches up its roots
Our bodies
        Stretched out
                Weigh no more than dawn
</pre>

[P.B.]

Madrigal

Más transparente
Que esa gota de agua
Entre los dedos de la enredadera
Mi pensamiento tiende un puente
De ti misma a ti misma
                              Mírate
Más real que el cuerpo que habitas
Fija en el centro de mi frente

Naciste para vivir en una isla

La llave de agua

Adelante de Rishikesh
el Ganges es todavía verde.
El horizonte de vidrio
se rompe entre los picos.
Caminamos sobre cristales.
Arriba y abajo
grandes golfos de calma.
En los espacios azules
rocas blancas, nubes negras.
Dijiste:
        Le pays est plein de sources.
Esa noche mojé mis manos en tus pechos.

Madrigal

More transparent
Than this water dropping
Through the vine's twined fingers
My thought stretches a bridge
From yourself to yourself
                    Look at you
Truer than the body you inhabit
Fixed in the centre of my mind

You were born to live on an island

[E.W.]

The Key of Water

After Rishikesh
the Ganges is still green.
The glass horizon
breaks among the peaks.
We walk upon crystals.
Above and below
great gulfs of calm.
In the blue spaces
white rocks, black clouds.
You said:
        Le pays est plein de sources.
That night I laved my hands in your breasts.

[E.B.]

Custodia

El nombre
Sus   sombras
El hombre La hembra
El mazo   El gong
La i   La o
La torre   El aljibe
El índice   La hora
El hueso   La rosa
El rocío   La huesa
El venero   La llama
El tizón   La noche
El río   La ciudad
La quilla   El ancla
El hembro La hombra
El hombre
Su cuerpo de nombres
Tu nombre en mi nombre En tu nombre mi nombre
Uno frente al otro uno contra el otro uno en torno al otro
El uno en el otro
Sin nombres

Shrine

The name
Its   umbras
The man The woman
The hammer   The gong
The i   The o
The tower   The well
The pointer   The hour
The bone   The rose
The shower   The grave
The spring   The flame
The brand   The night
The river   The city
The keel   The anchor
The manwomb The wombman
The man
His body of names
Your name in my name In your name my name
One facing the other one against the other one around the other
The one in the other
Nameless

[M.B.]

131

Domingo en la isla de Elefanta

Imprecación

Al pie de las sublimes esculturas,
Desfiguradas por los musulmanes y los portugueses,
La multitud ha dejado un *picnic* de basura
Para los cuervos y los perros.
Yo la condeno a renacer cien veces
En un muladar,
               Como a los otros,
Por eones, en carne viva han de tallarlos
En el infierno de los mutiladores de estatuas.

Invocación

Shiva y Parvati:
               Los adoramos
No como a dioses,
               Como a imágenes
De la divinidad de los hombres.
Ustedes son lo que el hombre hace y no es,
Lo que el hombre ha de ser
Cuando pague la condena del quehacer.
Shiva:
        Tus cuatro brazos son cuatro ríos,
Cuatro surtidores.
                Todo tu ser es una fuente
Y en ella se baña la linda Parvati,
En ella se mece como una barca graciosa.
El mar palpita bajo el sol:
Son los gruesos labios de Shiva que sonríe;
El mar es una larga llamarada:
Son los pasos de Parvati sobre las aguas.
Shiva y Parvati:
               La mujer que es mi mujer
Y yo,
     Nada les pedimos, nada

Sunday on Elefanta

Imprecation

Down at the foot of the sublime sculptures,
Disfigured by the Mohammedans and by the Portuguese,
The multitude has left its litter,
Tiffin for the crows and the curs.
I damn it to a thousand reincarnations,
Each on a muck-heap
                  While those others,
Can be carved in living flesh, for aeons,
In the hell for defacers of statues.

Invocation

Shiva and Parvati:
                We worship you
Not as gods,
          As images
Of the godliness of men.
You are what man does and is not,
What he is to be
When he has served the sentence of labour.
Shiva:
        Your four arms are four rivers,
Four springs.
             All your being is a fountain
Wherein the lovely Parvati bathes,
Wherein she bobs like a graceful craft.
The sea palpitates under the sun:
The full lips of Shiva smiling;
The sea is a long sheet of flame:
Footsteps of Parvati over the waters.
Shiva and Parvati:
                The woman who is my wife
And I,
       Ask you nothing, nothing

Que sea del otro mundo:

Sólo

La luz sobre el mar,
La luz descalza sobre el mar y la tierra dormidos.

From the other world:

                    Only

Light on the sea,
Light barefoot on the sea and the land asleep.

[M.E.]

Cuento de dos jardines

Una casa, un jardín,
                    No son lugares:
Giran, van y vienen.
                    Sus apariciones
Abren en el espacio
                    Otro espacio,
Otro tiempo en el tiempo.
                              Sus eclipses
No son abdicaciones:
                    Nos quemaría
La vivacidad de uno de esos instantes
Si durase otro instante.
                         Estamos condenados
A matar al tiempo:
                    Así morimos,
Poco a poco.
              Un jardín no es un lugar:
Por un sendero de arena rojiza
                              Entramos
En una gota de agua,
                    Bebemos en su centro
Verdes claridades,
                    Ascendemos
Por la espiral de las horas
                         Hasta
La punta del día,
                Descendemos
Hasta
       La consumación de su brasa.
Ríos en la noche: fluyen los jardines.

Aquel de Mixcoac era un cuerpo
Cubierto de heridas,
                    Una arquitectura
A punto de desplomarse.
                         Yo era niño
Y el jardín se parecía a mi abuelo.
Trepaba por sus rodillas vegetales

Fable of Two Gardens

A house, a garden,
$\qquad$ Are no places:
They spin, come and go.
$\qquad\qquad$ Their apparitions
Unfold in space
$\qquad$ Other space
Other time within time.
$\qquad\qquad$ Their eclipses
Are no abdications:
$\qquad\qquad$ We would be scorched
By the living flame of one of those moments
If it lived a moment longer.
$\qquad\qquad$ Condemned
To kill time:
$\qquad$ Piecemeal
We die.
$\qquad$ A garden is no place:
By a footpath of russet sand
$\qquad\qquad$ We enter
A water-drop,
$\qquad$ We drink at its centre
Green clarities,
$\qquad$ We ascend
By the spiral of the hours
$\qquad\qquad$ Up to
The peak of daylight,
$\qquad\qquad$ We descend
Down to
$\qquad$ The consummation of its ember.
Rivers in the night: the gardens ebb away.

The garden of Mixcoac was a corpse
Covered with wounds;
$\qquad\qquad$ An architecture
Almost toppling over.
$\qquad\qquad$ I was a little boy
And the garden was like my grandfather.
I clambered round its verdant legs,

Sin saber que eran los mástiles de un barco
Varado.
      El jardín lo sabía:
Esperaba su destrucción como el sentenciado
El hacha.
        La higuera era la Madre,
La Diosa:
          Zumbar de insectos coléricos,
Los sordos tambores de la sangre,
              El sol
Y su martillo,
           El verde abrazo de innumerables brazos,
La incisión del tronco.
              El mundo se entreabrió:
Yo creí que había visto a la muerte
             Al ver
La otra cara del ser,
        La vacía:
El fijo resplandor sin atributos.

En la frente del Ajusco
             Se apiñan
Las confederaciones blancas
               Hasta no ser
Sino una masa cárdena:
            El galope negro del aguacero
Cubre todo el llano.
           Llueve sobre lavas.
México: sobre la piedra ensangrentada
             Danza el agua.
Meses de espejos.
        El hormiguero,
Sus ritos subterráneos:
            Inmerso en la luz cruel
Expiaba mi cuerpo-hormiguero,
             Espiaba
La febril construcción de mi ruina.
             Élitros
El afilado canto del insecto
        Corta yerbas secas.

Not knowing they were the masts of a ship
Grounded.
        The garden knew:
It waited for its destruction as the convict
Waits the axe.
           The fig-tree was Mother
And Goddess:
           The buzz of angered insects,
The deaf drums of blood,
                The sun
And its hammer,
           The green embrace of numberless arms,
The incision in the trunk.
                The world half-opened:
I believed I had seen death
              When I saw
The other face of being,
            The void:
The permanent featureless brilliance.

On the brow of the Ajusco
              Cluster
The white confederations
           Till nothing is
But a purple mass:
           The black gallop of downpour
Covers all the plain.
           Rains on the lava.
Mexico: over the bloodstained stone
              Dances the water.
Months of mirrors.
           The anthill,
Its subterranean rituals:
             Immersed in the cruel light
My ant-hill body purified,
           but there lurked
The feverish building of my ruin.
             The wings
And sharp songs of the insect
           Scythe the dry grass.

Luz, luz:
                    Substancia del tiempo y sus inventos.
Cactos minerales,
                         Lagartijas de azogue
En las bardas de adobe,
                              El pájaro
Que perfora el espacio,
                              Sed, tedio, tolvaneras:
Impalpables epifanías del viento.
Los pinos me enseñaron a hablar solo.
En aquel jardín aprendí a despedirme.

Después no hubo jardines.
                              Un día,
Como si regresara,
                    No a mi casa:
Al comienzo del Comienzo,
                              Llegué a una claridad,
Ancha,
         Construida
Para los juegos pasionales de la luz y el agua.
Dispersiones, alianzas:
                    Del gorjeo del verde
Al azul más húmedo   Al gris entre brasas
                    Al más llagado rosa
Al oro desenterrado   Al verde verde.
Esa noche me enfrenté al *nim*.
                              Sobre sus hombros
El cielo con todas sus joyas bárbaras.
                                        El calor
Era una mano inmensa que se cerraba.
                                   Se oía
El jadeo de las raíces,
                    La dilatación del espacio,
El desmoronamiento del año.
                              Con una máscara de polvo,
Armado de silencio,
                    El árbol no cedía.
Era grande como el monumento de la paciencia.
Era justo como la balanza que pesa instantes y siglos.
Casa de las ardillas, mesón de los mirlos.

Light, light:
                    Substance of time and its inventions.
Cactus of mineral,
                              Quicksilver lizards
In the adobe huts,
                         The bird
Piercing space,
                         Thirst, tedium, sandstorms:
Impalpable epiphanies of wind.
The pines taught me to talk to myself.
In that garden I learned to say good-bye.

Afterwards there were no gardens.
                                   One day,
As if I were returning,
                              Not to my house:
But to the beginning of Beginning,
                                   I reached a clarity,
Wide-open,
               Built
For the impassioned play of light and water.
Dispersions, alliances:
                         From the chirrup of green
To moister blue   To the grey between embers
               To more wounded rose
To gold disinterred   To the green greenness.
That night I confronted the *nim* tree.
                                   On its shoulders
The sky with all its barbarous jewels.
                                        The heat
Was an immense and closing hand.
                                        You could hear
The panting of roots,
                         The dilation of space,
The slow mouldering of the year.
                                   With a mask of dust,
Armoured with silence,
                              The tree did not yield.
Its greatness was like a monument of patience.
Its justice a balance weighing instants and centuries.
House of squirrels, hostelry of blackbirds.

Cabían

En sus brazos muchas lunas.

La fuerza

Es fidelidad;

El poder es acatamiento:

Nadie acaba en sí mismo.

Un todo cada uno

En otro todo,

En otro uno:

Constelaciones.

El enorme *nim* sabía su pequeñez.

A sus pies

Supe que estaba vivo,

Supe que morir es ensancharse,

Negarse es crecer.

Entre gula y soberbia,

Codicia de vida

O fascinación por la muerte,

La vía de en medio.

En la fraternidad de los árboles

Aprendí a reconciliarme,

No conmigo:

Con lo que me levanta y me sostiene y me deja caer.

Me crucé con una muchacha.

El pacto

Del sol de verano y el sol de otoño: sus ojos.

Partidaria de acróbatas, astrónomos, camelleros.

Yo de fareros, lógicos, sadúes.

Nuestros cuerpos se hablaron, se juntaron y se fueron.

Nosotros nos fuimos con ellos.

Era el monzón:

Cielos de yerba machacada

Y el viento en armas

En todas las encrucijadas.

Por la niña del cuento,

Marinera de un estanque en borrasca,

La llamé Almendrita.

No un nombre:

Un velero intrépido.

Llovía,

                              And its arms
Were the home of many moons.
                         Force
Is fidelity:
          Power, acceptance:
None ends in himself.
                    Each one a whole
In another whole,
               In another one:
                              Constellations.
The enormous *nim* knew its tininess.
                              At its feet
I learned I was alive,
                    I learned that death is self-extension,
And self-denial is growth.
                         Between gluttony and pride,
Hunger for life
               Or fascination with death,
The *via media*.
               In the brotherhood of the trees
I learned to reconcile myself,
                         Not with myself:
But with that which lifts me up and holds me up and lets me fall.

I met a girl.
          The pact
Of the sun of summer and the sun of autumn: her eyes.
A lover of acrobats, astronomers, camel-drivers.
I of lighthouse-keepers, logicians, and saddhus.
Our bodies spoke, and joined, and parted.
We parted with them.
                         It was monsoon:
Skies of pounded grass
                    And the wind in arms
At every crossroad.
                         After the girl in the fable,
The sailor-girl of the storm-tossed lake,
                              I called her Almendrita.
Not a name:
          A fearless skiff.
The rain fell,

La tierra se vestía y así se desnudaba,
Las serpientes salían de sus hoyos,
                              La luna
Era de agua,
            El cielo se destrenzaba,
                              Sus trenzas
Eran ríos desatados,
                    Los ríos tragaban pueblos,
Muerte y vida se confundían,
                        Amasijo de lodo y sol,
Estación de lujuria y pestilencia,
                              Estación del rayo
Sobre el árbol de sándalo,
                        Tronchados astros genitales
Pudriéndose
            Resucitando
                        En tu vagina,
                              Madre India,
India niña
          Empapada de savia, semen, jugos venenosos.

A la casa le brotaron escamas.
                              Almendrita:
Llama intacta entre el culebreo y el ventarrón,
En la noche de hojas de banano
                              Ascua verde,
Hamadríada,
            Yakshi:
                  Risas en el matorral,
Manojo de albores en la espesura,
                              Más música
Que cuerpo,
            Más fuga de pájaro que música,
Más mujer que pájaro:
                        Sol tu vientre,
Sol en el agua,
              Agua de sol en la jarra,
Grano de girasol que yo planté en mi pecho,
                              Ágata
Leonada,
        Mazorca de llamas en el jardín de huesos.

The earth became clothed and thus became naked,
Snakes slithered from their holes,
                                The moon
Was of water,
            The heaven let down her hair,
                                        Her tresses
Were unbound rivers,
                    The rivers devoured villages,
Death and life became as one,
                            Dough of mud and sunlight.
Season of rich lust and pestilence,
                            Season of thunderbolt
Over the sandalwood tree,
                        Torn, genital stars
Rotting,
        Resuscitating
                    In your vagina,
                                Mother India,
Maiden India,
            Soaked with sap and sperm, the venomous juices.

The house budded with scales.
                            Almendrita:
Flame intact between the wreathing and the gusts of wind,
In the night of banana leaves
                            The green ember,
Hamadryad,
            Yakshi:
                    Laughter in the thicket,
A tangle of whiteness in the dark glade,
                                    More music
Than body,
            More flight of birds than music,
More woman than bird:
                    The sun your belly,
Sun in the water,
                Water of sun in the pitcher,
A grain of sunflowerseed I planted in my breast,
                                        Agate
Lion-yellow,
            A head of corn aflame in the garden of bone.

Chuang Tseu le pidió al cielo sus luminarias,
Sus címbalos al viento,
                          Para sus funerales.
Nosotros le pedimos al *nim* que nos casara.
Un jardín no es un lugar:
                          Es un tránsito,
Una pasión:
                No sabemos hacia donde vamos,
Transcurrir es suficiente,
                          Transcurrir es quedarse.
Una vertiginosa inmovilidad.
                          Estaciones
Como la sucesión de grandes reyes,
                          Cada invierno
Alta terraza sobre el año tendido.
                          Luz bien templada,
Resonancias, transparencias,
                          Esculturas de aire
Disipadas apenas pronunciadas,
                          ¡Sílabas,
Islas afortunadas!
                Engastado en la yerba,
El gato Demóstenes
                Es un carbón luminoso,
La gata Semíramis persigue quimeras,
                          Acecha
Reflejos, sombras, ecos.
                Arriba:
Sarcasmos de cuervos,
                El urogallo y su hembra:
Taciturnos príncipes desterrados,
                La upupa:
Pico y penacho un alfiler engalanado,
La verde artillería de los pericos fulgurantes,
La inmovilidad del milano
                          Negro
En el cielo sin escollos.
                Geometrías aéreas,
Veloces constelaciones en pleno día.
                Ahora,

Chuang Tseu begged of the sky its luminous stars,
Begged of the wind its cymbals,
                                    For his exequies.
We beg the *nim* to marry us.
A garden is no place:
                        It is a transition,
A passion:
                We know not where we go,
To elapse is enough,
                        To elapse is to remain.
A giddying immobility.
                        Seasons
Like the succession of great kings,
                                    Every winter
A high terrace above the unfolding year.
                                        Well-tempered light,
Resonances, transparencies,
                            Sculptures of air
No sooner pronounced than gone,
                                    Syllables,
The fortunate isles!   .
                        Encrusted in the grass
Demosthenes the cat
                    Is a glowing coal,
The she-cat Semiramis chases chimaeras,
                                        Lies in wait for
Shadows, echoes, reflections.
                        Overhead:
The sarcasms of crows,
                        The guinea-cock and his hen:
Taciturn exiled princes,
                        The hoopoe:
Beak and crest a decorated brooch,
The green artillery of dazzling parrots,
The stillness of the kite
                        Black
In the unhindering sky.
                        Aerial geometries,
Swift constellations at the height of day.
                                    Now,

Quieto
      Sobre la arista de una ola:
                      Un albatros,
Instantáneo peñasco de espuma que se dispersa.
No estamos lejos de Durban
                (Allí estudió Pessoa.)
Cruzamos un petrolero.
               Iba a Mombasa,
Ese puerto con nombre de fruta.
                (En mi sangre
Asamblea de estelas:
          Camoens, Vasco de Gama y los otros.)

El jardín se ha quedado atrás.
            ¿Atrás o adelante?
No hay más jardines que los que llevamos dentro.
¿Qué nos espera en la otra orilla?
              Pasión es tránsito:
La otra orilla está aquí,
         Luz en el aire sin orillas:
Prajnaparamita,
        Nuestra Señora de la Otra Orilla.
Tú misma,
      La muchacha del cuento,
           La alumna del jardín.
Olvidé a Nagarjuna y a Dharmakirti
          En tus pechos,
En tu grito los encontré:
       Maithuna,
         Dos en uno,
Uno en todo,
      Todo en nada,
        ¡*Sunyata,*
Plenitud vacía,
      Vacuidad redonda como tu grupa!

      Sombras girando
      Sobre un charco de luz.
      Mergos y ¿peces?
Hélice de diecisiete sílabas
         Dibujada en el mar
No por Basho:

148

Still
    Over the edge of a wave:
                        An albatross,
A momentary vanishing pinnacle of spray.
We are not far from Durban
                  (There Pessoa studied.)
We pass a tanker.
               It was heading for Mombasa,
The port with a name of fruit.
                    (In my blood
A gathering of the wakes of ships:
                  Camoens, Vasco de Gama and the rest.)

The garden has been left behind.
                  Behind or ahead?
There are no gardens save those we carry within us.
What awaits us on the other shore?
                  Passion is transition:
The other shore is here,
               Light in the shoreless air:
Prajnaparamita,
             Our Lady of the Other Shore,
Thou Thyself,
          The girl of the fable,
                The pupil of the garden.
I forgot Nagarjuna and Dharmakirti
               In your breasts,
In your cry I met them:
           Maithuna,
              Two in one,
One in all,
      All in nothing,
         Sunyata,
Vacant plenitude,
        Round emptiness like your haunches!

       Shadows turning
       Over a pool of light.
       Cormorants and fish?
Propellers of seventeen syllables
          Sketched in the sea
Not by Basho:

Por mis ojos, el sol y los pájaros,
                              Hoy,
A eso de las cuatro,
                  A la altura de Mauritania.
Una ola estalla:
              Mariposas de sal:
                              Desvanecimientos.
Metamorfosis de lo idéntico.
                        A esta misma hora
Delhi y sus piedras rojas,
                      Su río oscuro,
Sus domos blancos,
                  Sus siglos en añicos,
Se transfiguran:
                Arquitecturas sin peso,
                              Cristalizaciones
Casi mentales,
              Altos vértigos sobre un espejo.
Espiral de transparencias.
                        Se abisma
El jardín en una identidad
                        Sin nombre
Ni sustancia.
            Los signos se borran: yo miro la claridad.

Altamar, a bordo del Victoria *entre*
Bombay y Las Palmas, del 20 al 28
noviembre de 1968

By my eyes, the sun and the birds,
                                Today
At about four,
                To the heights of Mauritania.
The splash of a wave:
                        Butterflies of salt:
                                        Vanishings.
Metamorphosis of the identical.
                                At that same hour
Delhi and her red stones,
                        Her dark river,
Her white domes,
                    Her shattered centuries,
Are transfigured:
                    Weightless architectures,
                                        Crystallizations
Seemingly cerebral,
                    Lofty vertigos above a looking-glass.
Spiral of transparencies.
                        The garden
Plunges into its own abyss,
                        Into an identity
                                    Without name
Or substance.
                The signs are blotted out: I stare into clarity.
                                        [J.H. and E. C.-T.]

At sea on board the Victoria, *between*
Bombay and Las Palmas, 20 to 28 November 1968

from *Vuelta* (1976)

A vista de pdjaro

A Guillermo Sucre

Furiosamente
        Gira
Sobre un reflejo
           Cae
En línea recta
          Afilada
Blancura
      Asciende
Ya sangriento el pico
Sal dispersa
         Apenas línea
Al caer
    Recta
Tu mirada
       Sobre esta página
Disuelta

Bird's Eye View

To Guillermo Sucre

Furiously
       It whirls round
Over a reflection
             Falls
In a straight line
              Clear-cut
Whiteness
        Ascends
The beak now blood-red
Scattered salt
           Scarcely a line
As it falls
       Straight
Your glance
         Over this page
Dissolved

[C.T.]

Por la calle de Galeana

Golpean martillos allá arriba
      voces pulverizadas
Desde la punta de la tarde bajan
      verticalmente los albañiles

Estamos entre azul y buenas noches
      aquí comienzan los baldíos
Un charco anémico de pronto llamea
      la sombra del colibrí lo incendia

Al llegar a las primeras casas
      el verano se oxida
Alguien ha cerrado la puerta   alguien
      habla con su sombra

Pardea ya no hay nadie en la calle
      ni siquiera este perro
asustado de andar solo por ella
      Da miedo cerrar los ojos

Mexico, a 18 de junio de 1971

Along Galeana Street

Hammers pound there above
      pulverized voices
From the top of the afternoon
      the builders come straight down

We're between blue and good evening
      here begin vacant lots
A pale puddle suddenly blazes
      the shade of the hummingbird ignites it

Reaching the first houses
      the summer oxidizes
Someone has closed the door   someone
      speaks with his shadow

It darkens   There's no one in the street now
      not even this dog
scared to walk through it alone
      One's afraid to close one's eyes

Mexico, 18 June 1971

[E.B.]

Objetos y apariciones

A Joseph Cornell

Exaedros de madera y de vidrio
apenas más grandes que una caja de zapatos.
En ellos caben la noche y sus lámparas.

Monumentos a cada momento
hechos con los desechos de cada momento:
 aulas de infinito.

Canicas, botones, dedales, dados,
alfileres, timbres, cuentas de vidrio:
cuentos del tiempo.

Memoria teje y desteje los ecos:
en las cuatro esquinas de la caja
juegan al aleleví damas sin sombra.

El fuego enterrado en el espejo,
el agua dormida en el ágata:
solos de Jenny Lind y Jenny Colon.

'Hay que hacer un cuadro', dijo Degas,
'como se hace un crimen'. Pero tú construíste
cajas donde las cosas se aligeran de sus nombres.

Slot machine de visiones,
vaso de reencuentro de las reminiscencias,
hotel de grillos y de constelaciones.

Fragmentos mínimos, incoherentes:
al revés de la Historia, creadora de ruinas,
tú hiciste con tus ruinas creaciones.

Teatro de los espíritus:
los objetos juegan al aro
con las leyes de la identidad.

Objects and Apparitions

To Joseph Cornell

Hexahedrons of wood and glass
scarcely bigger than a shoe-box,
with room in them for night and all its lights.

Monuments to every moment,
refuse of every moment, used:
cages for infinity.

Marbles, buttons, thimbles, dice,
pins, stamps, and glass beads:
tales of the time.

Memory weaves, un-weaves the echoes:
in the four corners of the box
shadowless ladies play at hide-and-seek.

Fire buried in the mirror,
water sleeping in the agate:
solos of Jenny Colon and Jenny Lind.

'One has to commit a painting', said Degas,
'the way one commits a crime'. But you constructed
boxes where things hurry away from their names.

Slot machine of visions,
condensation flask for conversations,
hotel of crickets and constellations.

Minimal, incoherent fragments:
the opposite of History, creator of ruins,
out of your ruins you have made creations.

Theatre of the spirits:
objects putting the laws
of identity through hoops.

Las apariciones son patentes.
Sus cuerpos pesan menos que la luz.
Duran lo que dura esta frase.

Grand Hotel Couronne: en una redoma
el tres de tréboles y, toda ojos,
Almendrita en los jardines de un reflejo.

Un peine es un harpa
pulsada por la mirada de una niña
muda de nacimiento.

El reflector del ojo mental
disipa el espectáculo:
dios solitario sobre un mundo extinto.

Joseph Cornell: en el interior de tus cajas
mis palabras se volvieron visibles un instante.

Cambridge, Massachusetts, a 12 de enero de 1974

The apparitions are manifest,
their bodies weigh less than light,
lasting as long as this phrase lasts.

The Grand Hotel Couronne: is a vial,
the three of clubs and, very surprised,
Thumbelina in gardens of reflection.

A comb is a harp strummed by the glance
of a little girl
born dumb.

The reflector of the inner eye
scatters the spectacle:
God all alone above an extinct world.

Joseph Cornell: inside your boxes
my words became visible for a moment.

Cambridge, Massachusetts, 12 January 1974

[E.B.]

Piedra blanca y negra

Sima
    siembra una piedra
en el aire
        La piedra asciende
Adentro
      hay un viejo dormido
Si abre los ojos
        la piedra estalla
remolino de alas picos
            sobre una mujer
que fluye
     entre las barbas del otoño
La piedra desciende
       arde
en la plaza del ojo
       florece
en la palma de tu mano
          habla
suspendida
     entre tus pechos
lenguajes de agua
       La piedra madura
Adentro
    cantan las semillas
         Son siete
Siete hermanas
      Siete víboras
Siete gotas de jade
      Siete palabras
dormidas
    en un lecho de vidrio
Siete venas de agua
      en el centro
de la piedra
    abierta por la mirada

White and Black Stone

Sima
     sows a stone
in the air
          the stone rises
Inside
     there is an old man sleeping
If he opens his eyes
                    the stone explodes
whirlwind of beaks and wings
                         on a woman
who flows away
               among the beards of autumn
The stone descends
                burns
in the plaza of the eye
                    flowers
in the palm of your hand
                    speaks
hanging
        between your breasts
languages of water
                The stone ripens
Inside
     the seeds are singing
                    They are seven
Seven sisters
            seven vipers
Seven drops of jade
                seven words
asleep
      in a riverbed of glass
Seven veins of water
                   in the centre
of the stone
         that the glance breaks open

                                        [C.T.]

Note: Sima, painter, Czech by birth.

163

El fuego de cada día

A Juan García Ponce

Como el aire
                    hace y deshace
sobre las páginas de la geología,
sobre las mesas planetarias,
sus invisibles edificios:
                                        el hombre.
Su lenguaje es un grano apenas,
pero quemante,
                            en la palma del espacio.

Sílabas son incandescencias.
También son plantas:
                                        sus raíces
fracturan el silencio,
                                sus ramas
construyen casas de sonidos.
                                                Sílabas:
se enlazan y se desenlazan,
                                        juegan
a las semejanzas y las desemejanzas.

Sílabas:
            maduran en las frentes,
florecen en las bocas.
                                Sus raíces
beben noche, comen luz.
                                        Lenguajes:
árboles incandescentes
de follajes de lluvias.

Vegetaciones de relámpagos,
geometrías de ecos:
sobre la hoja de papel
el poema se hace
                            como el día
sobre la palma del espacio.

The Daily Fire

To Juan Garcia Ponce

As air
on the pages of geology,
on the planetary mesas,
makes unmakes
its invisible buildings:
                              man.
His language scarcely a seed
but burning
               in the palm of space.

Syllables are incandescences.
They are plants also:
                              their roots
fracture silence,
                         their branches
build houses of sound.
                              Syllables:
they bind unbind,
                    they play
at likeness and unlikeness,

Syllables:
         they ripen in brows,
they flower in mouths.
                              Their roots
drink night, eat light.
                              Languages:
incandescent trees
of rain foliage.

Vegetation of lightning,
geometries of echoes:
on the sheet of paper
the poem makes itself
                         as day
on the palm of space.

[O.P. and C.T.]

A la mitad de esta frase

No estoy en la cresta del mundo.
                              El instante
no es columna de estilita,
                       no sube
desde mis plantas el tiempo,
                         no estalla
en mi cráneo en una silenciosa explosión negra,
iluminación idéntica a la ceguera.
Estoy en un sexto piso,
                       estoy
en una jaula colgada del tiempo.

Sexto piso:
           marea y martilleo,
pelea de metales,
                 despeñavidrierío,
motores con rabia ya humana.
                            La noche
es un rumor que se desgaja,
                          un cuerpo
que al abrazarse se desgarra.
                            Ciega,
religa a tientas sus pedazos,
                            junta
sus nombres rotos, los esparce.
Con las remas cortadas
se palpa en sueños la ciudad.

No estoy en el crucero:
                       elegir
es equivocarse.
              Estoy
en la mitad de esta frase.
                          ¿Hacia dónde me lleva?

At the Mid-point of This Phrase

I am not on the wave crest of the world.
                                   The now
is not the stylite's column,
                         time
does not rise from my feet,
                              does not burst out in my skull
in a mute explosion of ebony,
a clarity identical with blindness.
                                   I am
on a sixth floor,
               I am
in a cage suspended from time.

Sixth floor:
                high tide and clatter,
metals battling,
                     broken glass hurled down,
engines, their rage already human.
                                   Night
is a self-destroying hubbub,
                         a body
rending itself with each self-embrace.
                                   Blindly,
it binds, groping, its fragments,
                              gathers
its broken names, re-scatters them.
With severed fingertips
the city feels itself in dreams.

I am not at the crossroad:
                         to choose
is to go wrong.
               I am
at the mid-point of this phrase.
                         Where is it leading me?

Retumba de tumbo en tumbo,
                              hechos y fechas,
mi nacicaída:
              calendario que se desmiembra
por las concavidades de mi memoria.
Soy el costal de mis sombras.

                              Declive
hacia los senos fláccidos de mi madre.
Colinas arrugadas,
                    lavadas lavas,
llano de llanto,
                 yantar de salitre.
Dos obreros abren el hoyo.
                            Desmoronada
boca de ladrillo y cemento.
                        Aparece
la caja desencajada:
                     entre tablones hendidos
el sombrero gris perla,
                         el par de zapatos,
el traje negro de abogado.
                            Huesos, trapos, botones:
montón de polvo súbito
                        a los pies de la luz.

Fría luz *no usada*,
                     casi dormida,
luz de la madrugada
                     recién bajada del monte,
pastora de los muertos.
                         Lo que fue mi padre
cabe en ese saco de lona
                          que un obrero me tiende
mientras mi madre se persigna.
                                Antes de terminarse
la visión se disipa:
                     estoy en la mitad,
colgado en una jaula,
                       colgado en una imagen.
El origen se aleja,
                   el fin se desvanece.

Echoes from stammer to stammer,
                              deeds and dates,
my birthfall:
             calendar that rips off its days
in my memory's hollowness.
I am my own sack of shadows.

                              Descent
towards my mother's flaccid breasts.
Wrinkled foothills,
                    laved lava,
plain of plaints,
                  the feast of lime.
Two workmen open the hole.
                              Crumbled
brick and mortar mouth.
                        And there
the coffin splintered:
                       through split boards
the pearl-grey hat,
                    the pair of shoes,
the black suit of the lawyer.
                              Rags, buttons, bones:
heap of sudden dust
                    at the light's feet.

Cold light untouched,
                      almost asleep,
dawn light
           fresh arrival from the hills,
shepherdess of the dead.
                          What was my father
fits in that canvas sack
                          a workman hands me
as my mother signs herself with the cross.
                                     Before it's done
the vision dissipates:
                       I am at the mid-point,
suspended in a cage,
                     suspended in an image.
The origin withdraws,
                      the destination vanishes.

No hay fin ni principio:
                              estoy en la pausa,
no acabo ni comienzo,
                        lo que digo
no tiene pies ni cabeza.
                              Doy vueltas en mí mismo
y siempre encuentro
                        los mismos nombres,
los mismos rostros
                        y a mí mismo no me encuentro.
Mi historia no es mía:
                        sílaba de esa frase rota
que en su delirio circular
                              repite la ciudad, repite.

Ciudad, mi ciudad,
                        estela afrentada,
piedra deshonrada,
                        nombre escupido,
Tu historia es la Historia:
                              destino
enmascarado de libertad,
                              estrella
errante y sin órbita,
                        juego
que todos jugamos sin saber las reglas,
juego que nadie gana,
                        juego sin reglas,
desvarío de un dios especulativo,
                              un hombre
vuelto dios tartamudo.
                        Nuestros oráculos
son los discursos del afásico,
                              nuestros profetas
son videntes con anteojos.
                        Historia:
ir y venir sin fin, sin comienzo.

There is neither end nor origin:
                              I am in the pause,
I do not finish and do not begin,
                              what I say
lacks both feet and head.
                              I turn and turn inside myself
and always come upon
                              the same names,
the same faces,
                    and I never come upon myself.
My history is not mine:
                         a syllable of that broken phrase
which in its round delirium
                              the city says again, again.

City, my city:
                    affronted stele,
dishonoured stone,
                    spat name.
Your history is History:
                              destiny
masked as liberty,
                    star
without course or orbit,
                         game
we all play ignorant of the rules,
game that no one wins,
                         game without rules,
whim of a speculating god,
                              a man
become a stammering god.
                              Our oracles
are the discourse of the aphasic,
                              our prophets
are seers with spectacles.
                         History:
come and go, endless, sourceless.

Nadie ha ido allá,
                    nadie
ha bebido en la fuente,
                          nadie
ha abierto los párpados de piedra del tiempo,
                                          nadie
ha oído la primera palabra,
                          nadie oirá la última,
la boca que la dice habla a solas,
                              nadie
ha bajado al hoyo de los universos,
                                nadie
ha vuelto del muladar de soles.

                          Historia:
basurero y arco iris.
                    Escala
hacia las altas terrazas:
                        siete notas
desvanecidas en la claridad.
                          Palabras sin sombra.
No las oímos, las negamos,
                          dijimos que no existían:
nos quedamos con el ruido.
                          Sexto piso:
estoy en la mitad de esta frase:
                              ¿hacia
dónde me lleva?
                    Lenguaje despedazado.
Poeta: jardinero de epitafios.

No one has gone there,
                    no one
has drunk at the fountain,
                    no one
has parted time's stone eyelids,
                         no one
has heard the first word,
                         no one will hear the last,
the mouth that says it mutters to itself,
                              no one
has penetrated the void of the universes,
                              no one
has come back from the dungheap of the suns.

                                        History:
dung-hill and rainbow.
                    Scale
up towards the high terraces:
                              seven notes
dissolved in clarity.
                    Shadowless words.
We did not hear them, we denied them,
                              said they could not be:
we chose the noise.
                    Sixth floor:
I am at the mid-point of this phrase:
                              where
is it taking me?
                    Mangled language.
Poet: tender of epitaphs.

                                             [M.S.]

Petrificada petrificante

Terramuerta
> terrisombra nopaltorio temezquible[1]

lodolsa cenipolva pedrósea[2]
> > fuego petrificado

cuenca vaciada
> el sol no se bebió el lago

no lo sorbió la tierra
> > el agua no regresó al aire

los hombres fueron los ejecutores del polvo
el viento
> se revuelca en la cama fría del fuego

el viento
> en la tumba del agua ·

recita las letanías de la sequía
> > el viento

cuchillo roto en el cráter apagado
> > > el viento

susurro de salitre

> El sol

anicorazol centrotal caledadoro[3]
> > > se partió

la palabra que baja en lenguas de fuego
> > > se quebró

el cuento y la cuenta de los años
el canto de los días
> > fue lluvia de chatarra

1. terrisombra = terri (torio) + sombra
   nopaltorio = nopal + (terri) torio
   temezquible = mezquite + temible = tem (ible) + mezqui (te) + tem (ible)
2. lodolsa = lodo + dolo + polvosa
   cenipolva = ceniza + polvo
   pedrósea = piedra + ósea (hueso)
3. anicorazol = ani(ma) + coraz(ón) + (s)ol. Anima – corazón – sol.
   centrotal = centr(al) + (t)otal. Central – total.
   calendadoro = cale(ntador) + dador + de oro. Dador de calor → dador de oro → edad de oro.

The Petrifying Petrified

Deadland
      Shadeadland cactideous nopalopolis[1]
dusht bonestony mockedmire[2]
                empty socket
petrified fire
      the sun did not drink the lake
the earth did not absorb it
          the water did not vanish in the air
men were the executors of the dust
wind
   swirled in the cold bed of fire
wind
   chanted litanies of drought
in the tomb of water
        wind
broken knife in the worn crater
         wind
saltpetre whisper

      The sun
solaortasoul centrotal soldonage[3]
         split
the word that came down in tongues of fire
            smashed
the account and the count of the years
the chant of the days
        was a rain of scrap iron

---

1. Shadeadland: shade/shaded + dead + land
   cactideous: cactus + hideous + cactus
   nopalopolis: nopal + polis
2. dusht: dust + ash
   bonestony: bone + nest + stony (4 syllables)
   mockedmire: mocked + mire, mock-admire (4 syllables)
3. solaortasoul: solar + aorta + soul
   centrotal: central + total
   soldonage: solar + donor + age (rhymes, more or less, with 'golden
   age')

pedregal de palabras
                          silabarios de arena
gritos machacados
                          talómordaz afrenoboz alrronzal[1]
caídos caínes neblinosos
                          abeles en jirones
sectarios sicarios
                    idólatras letrados
ladinos ladrones
                    ladridos del can tuerto
el guía de los muertos
                          perdido
en los giros del Ombligo de la Luna

Valle de México
                    boca opaca
lava de bava
                desmoronado trono de la Ira
obstinada obsidiana
                          petrificada
petrificante
            Ira
                torre hendida
talla larga como un aullido
                          pechos embadurnados
frente enfoscada
                    mocosangre verdeseca
                                      Ira
fijeza clavada en una herida
                          iranavaja cuchimirada[2]
sobre un país de espinas y de púas

                                Circo de montes
teatro de las nubes
                    mesa del mediodía
estera de la luna
                jardín de planetas

1. talón/mordaza/freno/bozal/ronzal
2. ira + navaja
   cuchillo + mirada

176

slagheap of words
                    sand primers
crushed screams
                    hoofmuz zlebridlehar nessbit[1]
whining waning Cains
                        Abels in rubble
partisan assasins
                    pagan pedagogues
slick crooks
            the woofs of the one-eyed dog
guide of the dead
                lost
in the coils of the Navel of the Moon

Valley of Mexico
                    lips in eclipse
lava slobber
            Rage's rotten throne
obstinate obsidian
                    petrified
petrifying
        Rage
            broken tower
tall as a scream
                smeared breasts
furious face
            greendry snotblood
                            Rage
nailed in a wound
                ragerazor gazeblade[2]
on a land of tines and spines

                        Circus of mountains
theatre of clouds
                    table of noon
mat of the moon
                    garden of planets

1. hoofmuz zlebridlehar nessbit: hoof + muzzle + bridle + harness +
   bit
2. ragerazor: rage + razor, rage-eraser (4 syllables)
   gazeblade: gaze + blade

tambor de la lluvia
                          balcón de las brisas
silla del sol
                  juego de pelota de las constelaciones
Imágenes reventadas
                          imágenes empaladas
salta la mano cortada
                          salta la lengua arrancada
saltan los senos tronchados
                          la verga guillotinada
tristrás en el polvo tristrás
                          en el patio trasero
podan el árbol de sangre
                          el árbol inteligente

Polvo de imágenes disecadas
                          La Virgen
corona de culebras
                  El Desollado
El Flechado
                  El Crucificado
El Colibrí
                  chispa con alas
tizónflor[1]
            La Llama
que habla con palabras de agua
                              La Señora
pechos de vino y vientre de pan
                              horno
donde arden los muertos y se cuecen los vivos
La Araña
            hija del aire
en su casa de aire
                          hila la luz
hila los días y los siglos
                          El Conejo
viento
        esculpido en el espejo de la luna

1. tizón + flor

178

drum of rain
            balcony of breezes
seat of the sun
                ball–game of the constellations
Bursting images
               impaled images
the lopped hand leaps
                    the uprooted tongue leaps
the sliced breasts leap
                the guillotined penis
over and over in the dust over and over
                          in the back courtyard
they trim the tree of blood
                the intelligent tree

Dust of dissected images
                The Virgin
crown of snakes
           The Flayed
The Felled-by-Arrows
              The Crucified
The Hummingbird
             winged spark
flowerbrand
         The Flame
who speaks with words of water
                  Our Lady
breasts of wine and belly of bread
                 oven
where the dead burn and the living bake
The Spider
         daughter of air
in her house of air
            spins light
spins centuries and days
           The Rabbit
wind
    carved in the mirror of the moon

                                        Imágenes enterradas
en el ojo del perro de los muertos
                              caídas
en el pozo cegado del origen
                                    torbellinos de reflejos
en el teatro de piedra de la memoria
                                    imágenes
girantes en el circo del ojo vaciado
                                    ideas
rojas verdes pardas
                        enjambre de moscas
las ideas se comieron a los dioses
                              los dioses
se volvieron ideas
                        grandes vejigas de bilis
las vejigas reventaron
                        los ídolos estallaron
pudrición de dioses
                        fue muladar el sagrario
el muladar fue criadero
                              brotaron ideas armadas
idearios ideodioses[1]
                        silogismos afilados
caníbales endiosados
                        ideas estúpidas como dioses
perras rabiosas
                        perras enamoradas de su vómito

Hemos desenterrado a la Ira
El anfiteatro del sol genital es un muladar
La fuente del agua lunar es un muladar
El parque de los enamorados es un muladar
La biblioteca es una madriguera de ratas feroces
La universidad es el charco de las ranas
El altar es la tramoya de Chanfalla
Los cerebros están manchados de tinta
Los doctores discuten en la ladronera
Los hombres de negocios
manos rápidas pensamientos lentos
ofician en el santuario

1. ideas + dioses. Dioses vueltos ideas.

                                    Images
buried in the eye of the dog of the dead
                                            fallen
into the overgrown well of origins
                                    whirlwinds of reflections
in the stone theatre of memory
                                    images
whirling in the circus of the empty eye
                                    ideas
of red brown green
                        swarms of flies
ideas ate the deities
                        deities
became ideas
            great bladders full of bile
the bladders burst
                    the idols exploded
putrefaction of the deities
                            the sanctuary was a dungheap
the dungheap a nursery
                        armed ideas sprouted
ideolized ideodeities
                    sharpened syllogisms
cannibal deities
                ideas idiotic as deities
rabid dogs
            dogs in love with their own vomit

We have dug up Rage
The amphitheatre of the genital sun is a dungheap
The fountain of lunar water is a dungheap
The lovers' park is a dungheap
The library is a nest of killer rats
The university is a muck full of frogs
The altar is Chanfalla's swindle
The brains are stained with ink
The doctors dispute in a den of thieves
The businessmen
fast hands   slow thoughts
officiate in the graveyard

Los dialécticos exaltan la sutileza de la soga
Los casuistas hisopean a los sayones
Amamantan a la violencia con leche dogmática
La idea fija se emborracha con el contra
El ideólogo cubiletero
                              afilador de sofismas
en su casa de citas truncadas
trama edenes para eunucos aplicados
bosque de patíbulos paraíso de jaulas
                    Imágenes manchadas
            escupieron sobre el origen
        carceleros del futuro   sanguijuelas del presente
        afrentaron el cuerpo vivo del tiempo
            Hemos desenterrado a la Ira

Sobre el pecho de México
                              tablas escritas por el sol
escalera de los siglos
                              terraza espiral del viento
baila la desenterrada
                    jadeo sed rabia
pelea de ciegos bajo el mediodía
                                  rabia sed jadeo
se golpean con piedras
                    los ciegos se golpean
se rompen los hombres
                    las piedras se rompen
adentro hay un agua que bebemos
                              agua que amarga
agua que alarga más la sed

                    ¿Dónde está el agua otra?

NOTES

Stanza 1. The Valley of Mexico. From lake to desert through the work of man.

Stanza 2. Mexico City, Discord: the degradation of the word in ideology. *The one-eyed dog*: according to Nahuatl mythology, the dead on their journey through the hells were guided by a dead dog – Quetzalcoatl's double.
Navel of the Moon: one of the possible etymologies for Mexico. The lake was called Navel of the Moon.

Stanza 4. The Ballgame, besides being a sport, was a rite of astronomical significance: the battle of the stars.

The dialecticians exalt the subtlety of the rope
The casuists sprinkle thugs with holy water
nursing violence with dogmatic milk
The fixed idea gets drunk with its opposite
The juggling ideologist
      sharpener of sophisms
in his house of truncated quotations *
plots Edens for industrious eunuchs
forest of gallows paradise of cages
     Stained images
    spit on the origins
   future jailers present leeches
  affront the living body of time
   We have dug up Rage

On the chest of Mexico
      tablets written by the sun
stairway of centuries
      spiral terrace of wind
the disinterred dances
     anger panting thirst
the blind in combat beneath the noon sun
       thirst panting anger
beating each other with rocks
     the blind are beating each other
the men are crushing
    the stones are crushing
within there is a water we drink
     bitter water
water whetting thirst

    Where is the other water?   [E.W.]

*house of truncated quotations: *or* house of truncated assignations.

Stanza 5. Allusions to various pre-Colombian gods and myths, and also
 to popular modern beliefs, especially the Virgin of Guadelupe (Our
 Lady with breasts of wine and belly of bread, oven where the living are
 created, pit where the dead are buried, etc).
Stanza 6. Myths, gods, images turned into ideology and journalistic
 notions.
Stanza 7. Modern Mexico. The businesses. The ideological struggle.
Stanza 8. The disinterred is Rage, the petrifying petrified.

             [O.P.]

Vuelta

A José Alvarado

Mejor será no regresar al pueblo,
al edén subvertido que se calla
en la mutilación de la metralla.

RAMÓN LÓPEZ VELARDE

Voces al doblar la esquina
               voces
entre los dedos del sol
                  sombra y luz
casi líquidas
           Silba el carpintero
silba el nevero
            silban
tres fresnos en la plazuela
                  Crece
se eleva el invisible
follaje de los sonidos
               Tiempo
tendido a secar en las azoteas
Estoy en Mixcoac
              En los buzones
se pudren las cartas
               Sobre la cal del muro
la mancha de la buganvilla
                   aplastada por el sol
escrita por el sol
              morada caligrafía pasional
Camino hacia atrás
             hacia lo que dejé
o me dejó
         Memoria
inminencia de precipicio
                balcón
sobre el vacío

Return

To José Alvarado

> It's better not to go back to the village,
> the subverted paradise silent
> in the shatter of shrapnel.
>
> RAMÓN LÓPEZ VELARDE

Voices at the corner's turn
                    voices
through the sun's spread hand
                        almost liquid
shadow and light
               The carpenter whistles
the iceman whistles
                 three ash trees
whistling in the plaza
                  The invisible
foliage of sounds growing
rising up
        Time
stretched to dry on the rooftops
I am in Mixcoac
              Letters rot
in the mailboxes
              The bougainvillea
against the wall's white lime
                    flattened by the sun
a stain a purple
             passionate calligraphy
written by the sun
I am walking back
               back to what I left
or to what left me
             Memory
edge of the abyss
           balcony
over the void

Camino sin avanzar
estoy rodeado de ciudad
                        Me falta aire
me falta cuerpo
                me faltan
la piedra que es almohada y losa
la yerba que es nube y agua
Se apaga el ánima
                Mediodía
puño de luz que golpea y golpea
Caer en una oficina
                        o sobre el asfalto
ir a parar a un hospital
                        la pena de morir así
no vale la pena
                Miro hacia atrás
ese pasante
            ya no es sino bruma

Germinación de pesadillas
infestación de imágenes leprosas
en el vientre los sesos los pulmones
en el sexo del templo y del colegio
en los cines
                impalpables poblaciones del deseo
en los sitios de convergencia del aquí y el allá
el esto y el aquello
                        en los telares del lenguaje
en la memoria y sus moradas
pululación de ideas con uñas y colmillos
multiplicación de razones en forma de cuchillos
en la plaza y en la catacumba
en el pozo del solitario
en la cama de espejos y en la cama de navajas
en los albañales sonámbulos
en los objetos del escaparate
sentados en un trono de miradas

Madura en el subsuelo
la vegetación de los desastres

                    I walk and do not move forward
I am surrounded by city
                              I lack air
lack body
            lack
the stone that is pillow and slab
grass that is cloud and water
The soul goes out
                    Noon
pounding fist of light
To collapse in an office
                              or onto the pavement
to end up in a hospital
                              the pain of dying like that
isn't worth the pain
                    I look back
that passerby
            nothing now but mist

The germination of nightmares
infestation of leprous images
in the belly brains lungs
in the genitals of the college and the temple
in the movie houses
                    desire's ghost population
in the meeting-places of here and there
this and that
            in the looms of language
in memory and its abodes
teeming clawed and tusked ideas

swarms of reasons shaped like knives
in the catacombs in the plaza
in the hermit's well
in the bed of mirrors and in the bed of razors
in the sleepwalking sewers
in the objects in the store window
seated on a throne of glances

The vegetation of disasters
ripens beneath the ground

                    Queman
millones y millones de billetes viejos
en el Banco de México
                        En esquinas y plazas
sobre anchos zócalos de lugares comunes
los Padres de la Iglesia cívica
cónclave taciturno de Gigantes y Cabezudos
ni águilas ni jaguares
                            los licenciados zopilotes
los tapachiches
                    alas de tinta mandíbulas de sierra
los coyotes ventrilocuos
                            traficantes de sombra
los benémeritos
                    el cacomixtle ladrón de gallinas
el monumento al Cascabel y a su víbora
los altares al máuser y al machete
el mausoleo del caimán con charreteras
esculpida retórica de frases de cemento

Arquitecturas paralíticas
                        barrios encallados
jardines en descomposición
                            médanos de salitre
baldíos
            campamentos de nómadas urbanos
hormigueros gusaneras
                        ciudades de la ciudad
costurones de cicatrices
                        callejas en carne viva
Ante la vitrina de los ataúdes
                        Pompas Fúnebres
putas
    pilares de la noche vana
                        Al amanecer
en el bar a la deriva
                    el deshielo del enorme espejo
donde los bebedores solitarios
contemplan la disolución de sus facciones
El sol se levanta de su lecho de huesos
El aire no es aire

                    They are burning
millions and millions of old notes
in the Bank of Mexico
                        On corners and plazas
on the wide pedestals of public places
the Fathers of the Civic Church
a silent conclave of puppet buffoons
neither eagles nor jaguars
                      buzzard lawyers
locusts
        wings of ink   sawing mandibles
ventriloquist coyotes
                  peddlers of shadows
worthy citizens
             the cacomistle   thief of hens
the monument to the Rattle and its snake
the altar to the Mauser and the Machete
the mausoleum of the epauletted Cayman
rhetoric sculpted in phrases of cement

Paralytic architecture
                 stranded districts
rotting municipal gardens
                   mounds of saltpetre
deserted lots
         camps of urban nomads
ant-nests worm-farms
               cities of the city
thoroughfares of scars
            alleys of living flesh
Funeral Parlours
               by the coffin's show-window
whores
    pillars of vain night
                 At dawn
in the drifting bar
             thaws the enormous mirror
where the solitary drinkers
contemplate the dissolution of their faces
The sun rises from its bed of bones
The air is not air

                              ahoga sin brazos ni manos
        El alba desgarra la cortina
                              Ciudad
        montón de palabras rotas

                              El viento
        en esquinas polvosas
                              hojea los periódicos
        Noticias de ayer
                              más remotas
        que una tablilla cuneiforme hecha pedazos
        Escrituras hendidas
                              lenguajes en añicos
        se quebraron los signos
                              atl tlachinolli
                    se rompió
                              agua quemada
        No hay centro
                    plaza de congregación y consagración
        no hay eje
                    dispersión de los años
        desbandada de los horizontes
                              Marcaron a la ciudad
        en cada puerta
                    en cada frente
                              el signo $

        Estamos rodeados
                    He vuelto adonde empecé
        ¿Gané o perdí?
                    (Preguntas
        ¿qué leyes rigen 'éxito' y 'fracaso'?
        Flotan los cantos de los pescadores
        ante la orilla inmóvil
                              Wang Wei al Prefecto Chang
        desde su cabaña en el lago
                              Pero yo no quiero
        una ermita intelectual
        en San Angel o en Coyoacán)
                              Todo es ganancia
        si todo es pérdida

                    strangling without arms or hands
Dawn rips the curtains
                              City
heap of broken words

                         Wind
on the dusty corners
                              turns the papers
Yesterday's news
                         more remote
than a cuneiform tablet smashed to bits
Cracked scriptures
                         languages in pieces
the signs were broken
                              atl tlachinolli
                              burnt water was split   .
There is no centre
                    plaza of congregation and consecration
there is no axis
                    the years dispersed
horizons disbanded
                         They have branded the city
on every door
                    on every forehead
                              the $ sign

We are surrounded
                    I have gone back to where I began
Did I win or lose?
                    (You ask
what laws rule 'success' and 'failure'?
The songs of fishermen float up
from the unmoving riverbank
                              Wang Wei to the Prefect Chang
from his cabin on the lake
                              But I don't want
an intellectual hermitage
in San Angel or Coyoacán)
                              All is gain
if all is lost

Camino hacia mi mismo
hacia la plazuela
El espacio está adentro
no es un *edén subvertido*
es un latido de tiempo
Los lugares son confluencias
aleteo de presencias
en un espacio instantáneo
Silba el viento
entre los fresnos
surtidores
luz y sombra casi líquidas
voces de agua
brillan fluyen se pierden
me dejan en las manos
un manojo de reflejos
Camino sin avanzar
Nunca llegamos
Nunca estamos en donde estamos
No el pasado
el presente es intocable

I walk toward myself
toward the plaza
Space is within
it is not a subverted paradise
it is a pulse-beat of time
Places are confluences
flutters of beings
in an instantaneous space
Wind whistles
in the ash trees
fountains
almost liquid light and shadow
voices of water
shine   flow   are lost
a bundle of reflections
left in my hands
I walk without moving forward
We never arrive
Never reach where we are
Not the past
the present is untouchable

[E.W.]

Trowbridge Street

1

El sol dentro del día
                    El frío dentro del sol
Calles sin nadie
                    autos parados
Todavía no hay nieve
                    hay viento viento
Arde todavía
            en el aire helado
un arbolito rojo
Hablo con él al hablar contigo

2

Estoy en un cuarto abandonado del lenguaje
Tu estás en otro cuarto idéntico
O los dos estamos
en una calle que tu mirada ha despoblado
                                    El mundo
imperceptiblemente se deshace
                            Memoria
desmoronada bajo nuestros pasos
Estoy parado a la mitad de esta línea
no escrita

3

Las puertas se abren y cierran solas
                            El aire
entra y sale por nuestra casa
                        El aire
habla a solas al hablar contigo
                            El aire
sin nombre por el pasillo interminable
No se sabe quien está del otro lado

Trowbridge Street

1

Sun throughout the day
                    Cold throughout the sun
Nobody on the streets
                    parked cars
Still no snow
            but wind wind
A red tree
            still burns
in the chilled air
Talking to it I talk to you

2

I am in a room abandoned by language
You are in another identical room
Or we both are
in a street your glance has depopulated
                            The world
imperceptibly comes apart
                    Memory
decayed beneath our feet
I am stopped in the middle of this
unwritten line

3

Doors open and close by themselves
                            Air
enters and leaves our house
                        Air
talks to itself talking to you
                        Air
nameless in the endless corridor
Who knows who is on the other side?

                              El aire
da vueltas y vueltas por mi cráneo vacío
                                    El aire
vuelve aire todo lo que toca
                        El aire
con dedos de aire disipa lo que digo
Soy aire que no miras
No puedo abrir tus ojos
                        No puedo cerrar la puerta
El aire se ha vuelto sólido

4

Esta hora tiene la forma de una pausa
La pausa tiene tu forma
Tu tienes la forma de una fuente
no de agua sino de tiempo
En lo alto del chorro de la fuente
saltan mis pedazos
el fuí o el soy o el no soy todavía
Mi vida no pesa
                El pasado se adelgaza
el futuro es un poco de agua en tus ojos

5

Ahora tienes la forma de un puente
Bajo tus arcos navega nuestro cuarto
Desde tu pretil nos vemos pasar
Ondeas en el viento más luz que cuerpo
En la otra orilla el sol crece
                        al revés
Sus raíces se entierran en el cielo
Podríamos ocultarnos en su follaje
Con sus ramas prendemos una hoguera
El día es habitable

                                        Air
turns and turns in my empty skull
                              Air
turns to air everything it touches
                              Air
with air-fingers scatters everything I say
I am the air that you don't see
I can't open your eyes
                        I can't close the door
Air has turned solid

4

This hour has the shape of a pause
This pause has your shape
You have the shape of a fountain made
not of water but of time
My pieces bob
at the jet's tip
what I was   am   still am not
My life is weightless
                        The past thins out
The future   a little water in your eyes

5

Now you have a bridge-shape
Our room navigates beneath your arches
We watch it pass from your railing
You ripple with wind   more light than body
The sun on the other bank
                              grows in upside-down
Its roots buried deep in the sky
We could hide ourselves in its foliage
Build a bonfire with its branches
The day is habitable

6

El frío ha inmovilizado al mundo
El espacio es de vidrio
               El vidrio es de aire
Los ruidos más leves erigen
súbitas esculturas
El eco las multiplica y las dispersa
Tal vez va a nevar
Tiembla el árbol encendido
Ya está rodeado de noche
Al hablar con él hablo contigo

6

The cold has immobilized the world
Space is made of glass
                         Glass made of air
The lightest sounds build
quick sculptures
Echoes multiply and disperse them
Maybe it will snow
The burning tree quivers
surrounded now by night
Talking to it I talk to you

[E.W.]

Primero de enero

Las puertas del año se abren,
como las del lenguaje,
hacia lo desconocido.
Anoche me dijiste:
                    mañana
habrá que trazar unos signos,
dibujar un paisaje, tejer una trama
sobre la doble página
del papel y del día.
Mañana habrá que inventar,
de nuevo,
la realidad de este mundo.

Ya tarde abrí los ojos.
Por el segundo de un segundo
sentí lo que el azteca,
acechando
desde el peñón del promontorio
por las rendijas de los horizontes
el incierto regreso del tiempo.

No, el año había regresado.
Llenaba todo el cuarto
y casi lo palpaban mis miradas.
El tiempo, sin nuestra ayuda,
había puesto,
en un orden idéntico al de ayer,
casas en la calle vacía,
nieve sobre las casas,
silencio sobre la nieve.

Tú estabas a mi lado,
aún dormida.
El día te había inventado
pero tú no aceptabas todavía
tu invención en este día.
Quizá tampoco la mía.
Tú estabas en otro día.

January First

The year's doors open
like those of language,
toward the unknown.
Last night you told me:
                    tomorrow
we shall have to think up signs,
sketch a landscape, fabricate a plan
on the double page
of day and paper.
Tomorrow, we shall have to invent,
once more,
the reality of this world.

I opened my eyes late.
For a second of a second
I felt what the Aztec felt,
on the crest of the promontory,
lying in wait
for time's uncertain return
through cracks in the horizon.

But no, the year had returned.
It filled all the room
and my look almost touched it.
Time, with no help from us,
had placed
in exactly the same order as yesterday
houses in the empty street,
snow on the houses,
silence on the snow.

You were beside me,
still asleep.
The day had invented you
but you hadn't yet accepted
being invented by the day.
– Nor possibly my being invented, either.
You were in another day.

Estabas a mi lado
y yo te veía, como la hieve,
dormida entre las apariencias.
El tiempo, sin nuestra ayuda,
inventa casas, calles, árboles,
mujeres dormidas.

Cuando abras los ojos
caminaremos, de nuevo,
entre las horas y sus invenciones.
Caminaremos entre las apariencias,
daremos fe del tiempo y sus conjugaciones.
Abriremos acaso las puertas del día.
Entraremos entonces en lo desconocido.

Cambridge, Massachusetts, a 1 de enero de 1975

You were beside me
and I saw you, like the snow,
asleep among appearances.
Time, with no help from us,
invents houses, streets, trees
and sleeping women.

When you open your eyes
we'll walk, once more,
among the hours and their inventions.
We'll walk among appearances
and bear witness to time and its conjugations.
Perhaps we'll open the day's doors.
And then we shall enter the unknown.

Cambridge, Massachusetts, 1 January 1975

[E.B.]

Epilogue

Día

Arbol copioso cada día. Este
(cinco de julio) hora a hora se vuelve
invisible: árbol que se borra
y en follajes futuros se vuelca.
Coming to terms with day – light, water, stone –
our words extend a world of objects
that remains itself: the new leaves
gladden us, but for no reason of their own –
sino por ser exclamaciones vegetales,
onomatopeyas de celebración
de la química resurrección anual,
where evening already stains the finished page
and shadow absorbing shadow, day
is going down in fire, in foliage.

[O.P. and C.T.]

Day

Copious tree each day. This one
(July the fifth) grows hour by hour
invisible: a tree obliterated
to be freighted down with future leaves.
Coming to terms with day – light, water, stone –
our words extend a world of objects
that remains itself: the new leaves
gladden us, but for no reason of their own –
merely to be vegetable exclamations,
onomatopoeias of celebration
of the yearly chemical resurrection,
where evening already stains the finished page
and shadow absorbing shadow, day
is going down in fire, in foliage.

[C.T.]